As the kingdom of God advances forcefully in this season, aggressive spiritual warfare becomes more and more necessary. God has chosen Cindy Trimm as one of the generals to strategize our spiritual offensive and to engage the enemy. However, the army she leads must hear clearly from God as they go into battle. *The Prayer Warrior's Way* is designed to help us all to hear accurately from God in order to emerge victoriously. You will love this book!

—C. Peter Wagner
Vice President & Apostolic Ambassador
Global Spheres, Inc.

The Prayer Warrior's Way is one of the best books that I have read to help believers develop a successful and fulfilling prayer life. It is very well researched and has deep wells to draw from that give us wisdom from some of the greatest Christian sources on the subject. I love the way Cindy Trimm writes! It makes you feel like you are having an intimate conversation with her about God.

—Cindy Jacobs
Cofounder of Generals International

the

PRAYER WARRIOR'S WAY

CINDY TRIMM

CHARISMA
HOUSE

Most CHARISMA HOUSE BOOK GROUP products are available at special quantity discounts for bulk purchase for sales promotions, premiums, fund-raising, and educational needs. For details, write Charisma House Book Group, 600 Rinehart Road, Lake Mary, Florida 32746, or telephone (407) 333-0600.

THE PRAYER WARRIOR'S WAY by Cindy Trimm
Published by Charisma House
Charisma Media/Charisma House Book Group
600 Rinehart Road
Lake Mary, Florida 32746
www.charismahouse.com

Unless otherwise noted, all Scripture quotations are from the New King James Version of the Bible. Copyright © 1979, 1980, 1982 by Thomas Nelson, Inc. Nashville, Tennessee. All rights reserved.

Scripture quotations marked ESV are from the Holy Bible, English Standard Version. Copyright © 2001 by Crossway Bibles, a division of Good News Publishers. Used by permission.

Cover design by Justin Evans
Design Director: Bill Johnson
Manuscript Preparation: Rick Killian, www.killiancreative.com

Visit the author's website at www.trimminternational.org.

Library of Congress Cataloging-in-Publication Data:
Trimm, Cindy.
  The prayer warrior's way / Cindy Trimm. -- 1st ed.
    p. cm.
  Includes bibliographical references (p.   ).
  ISBN 978-1-61638-470-8 (case bound) -- ISBN 978-1-
61638-572-9 (e-book) 1. Prayer--Christianity. I. Title.
  BV210.3.T75 2011
  248.3'2--dc23

                                          2011024282

This publication is translated in Spanish under the title
Como un guerrero ora, copyright © 2011 by Cindy Trimm,
published by Casa Creación, a Charisma Media company. All
rights reserved.

12 13 14 15 16 — 9 8 7 6 5 4 3
Printed in the United States of America

CONTENTS

Lord, teach us to pray.
—LUKE 11:1

PREFACE

*Everything starts from prayer. Without asking God for love,
we cannot possess love and still less are we able to give it
to others. Just as people today are speaking so much about
the poor but they do not know the poor, we too cannot talk
so much about prayer and yet not know how to pray.*
—Mother Teresa[1]

*The more praying there is in the world the better the world
will be, the mightier the forces against evil everywhere.
Prayer, in one phase of its operation, is a disinfectant
and a preventative. It purifies the air; it destroys the
contagion of evil. Prayer is no fitful, short-lived thing. It
is no voice crying unheard and unheeded in the silence. It
is a voice which goes into God's ear, and it lives as long
as God's ear is open to holy pleas, as long as God's heart
is alive to holy things. God shapes the world by prayer.*
—Edward M. Bounds[2]

GOD CREATED HUMAN beings—men and women alike—so He would have someone with whom He could communicate and share life. He wanted someone to walk with in the cool of the day, someone with whom He could exchange ideas, discuss dreams, and troubleshoot the resolution of concerns and challenges. He wanted someone with whom He could hold a real conversation. He wanted someone who had goals and dreams—plans, visions, and purpose He would infuse into every fiber of his or her being—something unique to that person separate from every other being in the universe, even Himself.

Put simply, He wanted someone to love—and someone who would love Him. He wanted someone who longed to hear His wisdom and lived to rejoice with Him over the marvels of His creation. He wanted someone He could trust to share His secrets with, someone He could partner with, someone who would recognize the wisdom of His every word and perform it, blessing Him just as He longed to bless them.

In the same way He took a rib from Adam's side to make a soul mate for him, He took something of Himself and placed it within each of us. According to Ecclesiastes 3:11, He put "eternity in man's heart" (ESV)—a mysterious part of His essence that would not only fill this lifetime with wonder, but also continue to give our existence joy and meaning into perpetuity with Him. It is the divine quest within each of us driving us to know God and be fully known by Him. It is the longing to experience intimacy with God—the insatiable appetite in each of our hearts that is never satisfied without experiencing more and more of Him.

In the Garden of Eden this all seemed so natural and perfect, but then tragedy struck. Since there can be no true obedience without the opportunity for disobedience, God allowed Adam and Eve to choose to follow their own wisdom—even if it was a foolish thing to do—instead of His own. He had filled them with every good thing, but they became convinced that they would not be complete if they did not know evil as well as good. So they made the choice to partake of the tree of the knowledge of good *and* evil, and suddenly their continuous conversation with God was broken. God even had to come looking for them, calling out, "Where are you?" (Gen. 3:9), because it was the first time they did not immediately respond when He spoke to them. It was the first time He had sensed their separation from Himself. His once seamless communion with Adam and Eve had been severed, and it would take Jesus being sacrificed on the cross to repair the rift that now existed between heaven and earth.

Thus today we stand as heirs of promises beyond our wildest hopes and imaginings, but handicapped by being born into the constraints of this world with ears untrained to hear the pulse of heaven. We grow up thinking everything that exists is defined by what we see, touch, smell, taste, and hear with our physical senses. Our minds absorb it and are framed by it, even as the eternity in our hearts cries out for more—for a taste of the infinite. Why do you think stories about magic, superheroes, and miracles are so popular in our culture today? It is because there is something in us calling out for that which is beyond our day-to-day experience—our hearts are calling out for God and the supernatural, even though most have confused this desire with Superman, *The Lord of the Rings*, and *Star Wars*. We know in our deepest selves that there is a world more real out there than the Matrix we live in, but confused by the world's lies, too many of us settle for simple stories rather than taking on the quest of knowing the one true God—the only real answer to the call of eternity in our hearts.

You see, there's a conversation that has been going on from long before this universe was even created—a conversation taking place in the spiritual realm in the throne room of heaven. Before the fall of humanity, Adam and Eve were part of it, and there is something buried in each of our hearts that tells us we were created to be part of it as well. It's a dialogue built into the very fabric of our DNA. We long for it. We yearn to be in on it. But despite giving our lives to Christ and being born again in the Spirit, we still don't know how to plug into it.

We get small snippets of that big conversation from time to time as we pray, read the Bible, or open our hearts in worship, but they are seldom more than cryptic messages that we don't fully understand. We thrill on the inside at the slight glimpses of the "other world," even as they confuse us. We get frustrated that we do not have a more complete picture—and more often than not, we get discouraged and fall away from prayer as if it were nothing more than a time-consuming exercise in spiritual contemplation and meditation. Rather than plunging into the life in the Spirit God is ever trying to open to us, we fall back into operating as natural beings confined by the laws of the natural world rather than those of the spirit.

In my book *The Art of War for Spiritual Battle*, I laid out the framework for what this big conversation is all about using examples of some who have gone before us and fully participated in it—the Charles Finneys, Jeanne Guyons, John Wesleys, William and Catherine Booths, William Seymours, and Rees Howells of history who not only heard from heaven, but like Abraham, David, and Paul also partnered with God to change their age. They were generals of prayer who engaged the enemy and employed the strategies of heaven to transform their world.

But before these heroes of the faith were generals, they were common foot soldiers like you and me. What made the difference for them? What were the qualities and practices that propelled them into God's inner circle of trusted confidantes and advisers? What did they do to become friends of God like the patriarchs of the Old Testament and those in the Book of Acts who "turned the world upside down" (Acts 17:6)? What caused them to again walk like Adam and Eve continually in conversation with the Father of all creation?

As *The Art of War for Spiritual Battle* was a vision of what is possible on the earth when we connect with the strategic high command of heaven's throne room, *The Prayer Warrior's Way* is a field manual for the common foot soldiers who need to learn to hear from heaven for themselves. This book provides basic training in God's boot camp of prayer and life after the Spirit. Before you can be a privileged confidante and adviser fully participating in the big conversation of heaven, you must first learn to do battle in the trenches of your own personal life and the world it touches. Before you can pray for the building of a five-thousand-seat church, you must first learn to successfully pray to cover your rent or mortgage. You will never know how to win your city for Jesus until you know how to pray your neighbors and your family into the kingdom. As God told Jeremiah, "If you have run with the footmen, and they have wearied you, then how can you contend with horses?" (Jer. 12:5). You will never hear the strategies of heaven for your nation until you know how to hear the plans and purposes of heaven for your own life.

All of this starts with you, in your prayer closet, laying your heart and your requests before the throne of heaven, *every day*. If you can't get a word from heaven for today, how do you expect to get the plan of heaven for this year? For your lifetime? For your city, your nation, or your world? How will you learn the things God wants you to know about who you are in His kingdom and what He has for you to do in it?

Believe it or not, God has things He is trying to say to you *right now*, but if you are like most people, you don't know how to hear them. You are not yet versed in the prayer basics necessary for hearing from God for yourself. That is why I have written this book as a follow-up to *The Art of War for Spiritual Battle*. What is in these pages is what you need to know to be part of the most important conversation in the universe— the one going on in heaven about how to bring health, abundance, joy, and salvation to your world.

You see, God doesn't promote privates into generals overnight because He knows the risks. Authority without discipline is harmful for both leaders and followers. How often have we seen men and women rise up too quickly in the body of Christ only to crash and burn because they ran things the way the world does rather than how they were instructed from heaven? We are all called into ministry—whether it is as business people, teachers, doctors, lawyers, janitors, artists, legislators, or whatever else God has put on our hearts. There are as many different callings in the body of Christ as there are needs! While each calling takes a specific expertise and requires unique talents and gifts, they all have one thing in common: success is determined by one's ability to know how to pray and get direction from heaven.

It's all about decision making. Wouldn't you like to know the decision God wants you to make every time? Well, that is what *The Prayer Warrior's Way* is all about.

Are you ready to learn what you need to know in order to practice participating in the great conversation of heaven and earth? Then read on. God can't wait to get you in on the dialogue He's been planning to share with you since before you were born!

If you abide in Me, and My words abide in you, you will ask what you desire, and it shall be done for you. By this My Father is glorified, that you bear much fruit; so you will be My disciples.

—JOHN 15:7–8

Though in its beginnings prayer is so simple that the feeblest child can pray, yet it is at the same time the highest and holiest work to which man can rise. It is fellowship with the Unseen and Most Holy One. The powers of the eternal world have been placed at its disposal. It is the very essence of true religion, the channel of all blessings, the secret of power and life.... It is on prayer that the promises wait for their fulfillment, the kingdom for its coming, the glory of God for its full revelation.... [For] true prayer, that takes hold of God's strength, that availeth much, to which the gates of heaven are really opened wide—who would not cry, Oh for some one to teach me thus to pray?

—ANDREW MURRAY[3]

INTRODUCTION

Now it came to pass, as He was praying in a certain place,
when He ceased, that one of His disciples said to Him,
"Lord, teach us to pray, as John also taught his disciples."
—Luke 11:1

IMAGINE THIS SCENE for a moment. This is not the beginning of Jesus's ministry. In fact, because this is pretty much in the middle of the Book of Luke, it is likely the disciples had been walking, eating, and living with Jesus for some time now. They must have learned many of the nuances of Jesus's habits the same way you and I learn the individual quirks of siblings or roommates. They had certainly seen several miracles and heard some powerful teaching by this point. They had heard Jesus answer dozens of questions with astonishing wisdom and field the many cleverly veiled attempts to discredit Him without a single embarrassment. They had seen Him command storms, feed thousands, cast out demons, heal the sick, give sight to the blind, and raise the dead. They were getting a glimpse of the new kingdom He was telling them about and the power His words commanded. They knew that whatever He promised, He could perform.

And during this time, they experienced Jesus's dedication to prayer firsthand.

I am sure it wasn't uncommon for them to fall asleep waiting for Jesus to come back from prayer, or wake up to find Him gone off to some lonely place to get more personal time with His Father. At first it must have concerned them when He disappeared, but by this time they must have been able to surmise, "Oh, He's probably out praying again. Should we start breakfast? It could be awhile."

Waking to find Him gone this time, they probably whispered among themselves something like: "You know, Jesus does things that no one else has ever done, but He also prays like no one else we have ever known. He disappears for hours at a time every single day just so He can *pray*. It's as if prayer is more important to Him than we are! He skips meals to pray. He doesn't speak until He has prayed. In fact, He manages His entire schedule *around* His prayer time, not His prayer around all the other things He has to do! Even though we have been taught about prayer from the time we were children, there is something He must know about prayer that we don't. Do you think we could get Him to teach us to pray with the same effectiveness?"

And so, when He finally returned to them that morning, they asked Him, "Lord, teach us to pray."

Why? Because they knew that there was something in the way Jesus prayed that got answers.

So Jesus taught them:

> When you pray, say: Our Father in heaven, hallowed be Your name. Your kingdom come. Your will be done on earth as it is in heaven. Give us day by day our daily bread. And forgive us our sins, for we also forgive everyone who is indebted to us. And do not lead us into temptation, but deliver us from the evil one.
>
> —Luke 11:2–4

It was an outline for prayer—a disciple's prayer to address every need of every day. It was a place to start. But it wasn't all He had to offer—with the outline, the disciples also needed to come to prayer with the proper attitude and resolve, so He continued to teach them:

> Which of you shall have a friend, and go to him at midnight and say to him, "Friend, lend me three loaves; for a friend of mine has come to me on his journey, and I have nothing to set before him"; and he will answer from within and say,

"Do not trouble me; the door is now shut, and my children are with me in bed; I cannot rise and give to you"? I say to you, though he will not rise and give to him because he is his friend, yet because of his persistence he will rise and give him as many as he needs.

So I say to you, ask, and it will be given to you; seek, and you will find; knock, and it will be opened to you. For everyone who asks receives, and he who seeks finds, and to him who knocks it will be opened.

If a son asks for bread from any father among you, will he give him a stone? Or if he asks for a fish, will he give him a serpent instead of a fish? Or if he asks for an egg, will he offer him a scorpion? If you then, being evil, know how to give good gifts to your children, how much more will your heavenly Father give the Holy Spirit to those who ask Him!

—LUKE 11:5–13

In essence, Jesus was saying, "Who in need would come to the door, knock, and then go away without an answer? Even if the person were asking at the worst time possible, wouldn't he or she continue knocking until the need was met? Even if the individual were asking someone who was cantankerous and uncooperative, wouldn't he keep after the person until his need was met?

"You see, our Father is a good Father, and He wants you to have what you need. When you ask for one thing, He is not going to give you something that is of no use or might be harmful. But He's not a vending machine you can just pop a few coins into, get what you want, and then walk away from either. He wants a relationship with you. To have this, you must give Him what He wants—your heart. You must continue to knock and seek if you hope to find. You have to spend time sitting at His feet, letting Him teach and purify you. It is the only way you can cut through the static of your own mind in order to hear His answer.

"If you do that, He will not refuse you, nor will He withhold from you the most precious thing He has—His own Spirit—that you might be able to do and be all He desires for you. Do you have faith like an impertinent neighbor? Will you go to the door of heaven and keep knocking until you get what you need? Do you believe that when you go and knock you will hear an answer from the other side of the door? Because, I'm telling you here and now, if you don't keep after it, if you're unsure you will get an answer, if you are hesitant or grow frustrated, you will never get what you are after; but if you have patience and faith in prayer, there is nothing in heaven our Father won't make available to you."

The disciples had certainly seen Jesus's persistence in prayer, but the idea that they could go into prayer and then come back with the answer they needed was new. Certainly they were aware the patriarchs had prayed and conversed with God just as Adam and Eve had in the Garden of Eden, but they were special, weren't they? God had called them into those unique relationships with Himself. Could it really be that God wanted the same kind of relationship with each of them?

In the revolutionary disciple's prayer Jesus offered in this passage, He not only gave them an outline of what to pray for daily—a starting place for consistently knocking on the door of heaven—but also the means of transforming their own minds from men and women trapped in a world of doubt, oppression, and failure into a mind-set of heaven: one of faith, provision, and overcoming. He was not teaching them something to be repeated *ad nauseam* in church services and prayer closets, but a dynamic way to open hearts to the infinite and eternal each and every day. It is a meditation, a discipline, and a practice to let God speak into and through. It is as simple as saying the words from memory, but also as rich as taking each line—even each word—and letting God speak through them to develop in us the lifestyle and faith of someone who turns their world upside right.

In the following chapters I want to look at each of the parts of this prayer more closely and help you see the mystery God planted in each word for us to open up and put into action. Whether you were just born again yesterday, are a ministry leader, or have been leading prayer at your church for decades, I know there is something in the following pages that you haven't seen before that could be the key to the breakthroughs you have been struggling to see realized. God has the answers you need, and they are there for those who ask, seek, and knock without reprieve or shame.

I believe that as you read this book, just as happened as I studied to write it, that what is within these lines will transform your life in miraculous ways. God has so much He is trying to convey to you, but you must first become the person who can pray and hear His voice—one who can confidently follow the prayer warrior's way.

> Jesus never taught His disciples how to preach, only how to pray.
>
> —ANDREW MURRAY[1]

PART ONE

The Big Picture

Our Father in heaven, hallowed be Your name.
Your kingdom come. Your will be done
on earth as it is in heaven.
—MATTHEW 6:9–10

1

THE GREAT PARADIGM SHIFT
Turning Reality Inside Out

Our Father in heaven.
—Matthew 6:9

*If you then, being evil, know how to give good gifts to
your children, how much more will your Father who
is in heaven give good things to those who ask Him!*
—Matthew 7:11

*O*UR FATHER.

There is a spiritual revolution in those words.

Jesus didn't teach His disciples to start their prayers, "O God of Abraham and Isaac and Jacob and Moses," or "O Maker of heaven and earth," or even "O great Spirit who sees all and knows all," but *"Father"*—and not just "Father," but *"our* Father." He didn't start it with *"My* Father," so that people might mistakenly think it was supposed to be only "Jesus's Father," but *"Our Father,"* expressing the fact that "you are My brothers and sisters and God is *our* Father." Paul, who received the revelation of this, amplified what Jesus said here, explaining, "You received the Spirit of adoption by whom we cry out, 'Abba [we would say "Daddy"] Father.'" (Rom. 8:15).

It is what Jesus prayed in the garden as He asked that He might not have to suffer the cross in Mark 14:36. In essence, He asked, "Daddy? Father? I'll do whatever You want Me to do, but couldn't We save humanity some other way?" He was calling on the intimate relationship He shared with His "Daddy" while appealing to the authority of the head of His household, who was His "Father." Bowing His knee to each, He went to the cross, but because of the quality of His relationship with the One He could call "Daddy," He didn't go alone.

By instructing us to pray *"Our Father,"* Jesus told us we had the right to go to God in this same capacity. If you learn nothing else from this book, I want you to get your mind around this revelation: You are God's child, and He wants to have a relationship with you like a father to a son, a daddy to a daughter. God wants to hear your prayers and see that prayer develop in you the power of an overcomer. As Pete Greig, one of the founders and leaders of the 24-7 Prayer movement, described it:

> Prayer is about power. Prayer is about miracles. Prayer is about breakthrough. Prayer is about the extension of the kingdom. But more than any of that, prayer is about being intimate with God. It is about the lap of the Father, and being chosen by Jesus.[1]

The beginning of confidence in prayer is realizing that there is Someone on the other end who not only wants the best for you, but who also wants the same relationship with you that a parent has with a child. He wants to see you born whole, admiring your every little finger and toe; see you grow; see you learn to walk; see you learn to fend for yourself; and never be farther away than a phone call or a text message as you mature and go out to fulfill your purpose in the "family business." He wants to hear what you have to say; He wants to see your needs met; He wants to answer your questions; He wants to give you understanding, wisdom, and revelation; and He wants to meet your friends. He always has your back, He always has wise advice for you, He has words of encouragement and edification, and He has the power of the universe to use on your behalf when He sees fit. All you have to do is make the connection with Him.

Now I know this may be a hard concept for some of us to grasp, especially if our earthly fathers weren't exactly focused on "connection." Many fathers are absent—if not physically, then emotionally. I truly believe there has been an attack on fatherhood in our world for exactly this reason. The enemy doesn't want us to have a good opinion of fathers that might put us one step closer to God *the* Father. Satan wants us to think of fathers as guys who leave when we are too young to remember them, men who drink too much, who use their hands to beat us rather than train or comfort us, who are selfish and lazy, aimless and thieving, reckless, uncaring, destructive, and flawed.

As *The Shack* author William P. Young described this feeling: "I spent most of my life trying to wipe the face of my father off the face of God."[2] If that is what your father was like, I want you to lay that aside. I want you to let that mind-set be broken off of your life because it is a curse that doesn't belong to you. Your heavenly Father has none of those negative characteristics.

Instead I want you to imagine what the best father on earth would be like. Your heart knows more about real fatherhood than you may realize. God put a bit of Himself into each of us. Think of the good fathers you have read about in books and seen in the movies or experienced in the homes of your friends. What characteristics of those dads gave you clues as to what a truly good father is like? Take some time to imagine how the best possible father would be, and then think again because God is a Father above what we can ask for or imagine.

Meditate on the goodness of God the Father and let Him fill your thoughts with Himself. That is "our Father"—that is "your Father" and "my Father." That is the Father who created all of heaven and earth—the entire universe, in fact—just so we would have a place to play. That is the Father who planned out the best for you before you were even conceived in your mother's womb. Again, look at how Jesus describes "our Father":

> If your child asks for bread, do you trick him with sawdust? If he asks for fish, do you scare him with a live snake on his plate? As bad as you are, you wouldn't think of such a thing. You're at least decent to your own children. So don't you think the God who conceived you in love will be even better?
> —MATTHEW 7:9–11, THE MESSAGE

Even if you didn't have a good father, you still know on the inside what a good father would be like. While it may take awhile for these truths to be real to you, the beginning is in going to "our Father" in prayer. Go and sit in His presence and let Him teach you who He really is. Spend time sitting in His lap. He won't mind—in fact, it is what He has always hoped you would do!

GROWING UP WITH GOD

Once the revelation of God as Daddy and Father begins to sink into our awareness, the next thing we need to realize about prayer is that we have some growing up to do if we expect the communication to be two-way. Prayer monologues are easy—like grocery lists of needs or pages of memorized scriptures or books that prompt us to just insert our names and those of our loved ones into the blanks provided in prewritten prayers. I am not saying these are bad. I have written out such prayers and confessions myself, and find them very reassuring, positive, and transformational. Repeating such prayers and confessions are wonderful ways to reset our hearts about who God is and what He really wants for us. They are a key to unlocking the impossible, but they are not all that prayer is about.

Two-way prayer is something beyond all of that. It is asking God for or about something, and then receiving His answer. It is a conversation. Yet, in order for that conversation to take place, our spiritual ears must mature enough for us to discern God's voice from all of the others that speak into our heads and our lives. There is more to prayer than most people think. We must do work within ourselves in order to become mature enough to talk to our Father as a friend and partner.

When a baby is born, it doesn't really know how to do anything. The child's five senses may work perfectly, but the child has to learn what the input from those senses means. A child isn't born knowing that some things it sees are people, others furniture, and still others walls, doorways, or parakeets. The child doesn't know what to focus on. Babies have no depth perception. If you have ever held a newborn, you will notice its head and eyes wander randomly around as the child's brain begins the process of distinguishing one thing from another.

The first thing a baby learns to focus on is the face of the person holding him or her as that person coos and goo-goos and caresses his or her cheek. Babies learn to focus on their mother's face as they suckle or on their father's as he rocks them to sleep. They learn to distinguish noises from voices and words from gibberish. They learn what cries to make to gain attention and which gurgles to make to receive smiles and affection. It is a process that takes months and comes slowly, but the more the baby interacts with his or her parents, the faster he or she learns to know them. Is it really any different when we are born spiritually? If you remember when you were first born again, if you were anything like most new Christians, you became a sponge, soaking up everything you could learn about God and His spiritual world. With the miracle of spiritual birth still so close to your experience, everything about God seemed so vital, vibrant, and real. When you prayed, it was as if you could feel His breath on your face as He drew near. Answers to your requests seemed to come almost before they were out of your mouth! The new world of getting to know God was so full of wonder and excitement!

But as we mature, so do our relationships, both spiritually and physically. Eventually babies are expected to learn real words to get what they are after; they cannot just cry and think they will be given what they want. They must understand the words *no* and *don't* to avoid the things that might hurt them. Then they are expected to learn to obey instructions and recognize the voice of their parents over the voices of the world around them. As they learn to walk and move about on their own, they enter the world of "toddlerdom." They learn the power of willfulness and the rewards of obedience. This is the phase spiritually where I believe the vast majority of Christians gets stuck and stagnate.

Most of us have witnessed a toddler throwing a tantrum on the floor because the child didn't get what he or she wanted. Children do this because they remember crying out when they were only a few months old and seeing help come immediately. But when a child does this at three years old, crying doesn't achieve the same response. Suddenly mom and dad hang back for a bit, waiting for the child to calm down and "use words" because mommy and daddy don't understand what the child is asking for. Even though the parents or caregivers probably do know intuitively what the child wants, they cannot respond to the cries of a three-year-old in the same way they did for a three-month-old.

It is time for the child to grow up a little and start learning to respect others and self, to think about why he should have something rather than simply believing mom and dad should immediately respond to his every whim. The process is gradual, but the relationship between parent and child must change as time progresses if the child is ever to become a responsible, contributing, successful member of society. No matter what great plans parents have for their child, if a child never gets past the phase of kicking and screaming and thinking the entire world is centered around him, he will never near his potential as a human being.

That is the place I believe most of the church is today in our efforts to follow Jesus. We crave our own satisfaction and comfort more than we crave the voice of God. This is why we haven't yet learned to distinguish the voice of God from the voices of the rest of the world. We don't want to grow up and separate ourselves from the things that are holding us back. We want all the rewards of being a member of God's family, but we don't want to sacrifice our time in prayer and studying God's Word in order to grow up to the point where we could handle all He longs to give us.

Culture Shock

You see, the problem is when we grow up physically, we don't have the confusion of differing realities that we do when we grow up spiritually. It is perplexing when some of the voices we have speaking in our heads and making decisions for us are those of our own mind, will, and emotions. A physical baby has a mind that is also a baby physically, and a physical three-year-old typically has a mind that is also three years old. When a three-year-old personality speaks out of a three-year-old body, no one is fooled into thinking that the child has enough wisdom to be left totally to himself. We know to guide the child toward the right decisions and sometime still let him or her fall down when the lesson isn't too costly.

However, when a thirty-year-old physical mind brought up in this world starts contending with the three-year-old spiritual mind that God is trying to mature in the truths of the spiritual world, the thirty-year-old mind must be willing to humble itself and listen. If not, the spiritual voice can easily get ridiculed and overruled "because the carnal mind is enmity against God" (Rom. 8:7). As our spirits start to mature and God draws back from us enough to let us begin growing toward responsible citizenship in His kingdom, we are faced with the same problem as someone who relocates to a new country and culture.

We must either start conforming to the new culture, or things will repeatedly go wrong. We will have to learn a new language, a new way of doing things, and even a new way of thinking, or else we will never succeed in the new country no matter how well versed we are in the old.

This is the perplexity we have as beings with feet in two different realms: the culture and realm of this world—a place of limitations and lack, setbacks and failures, arrogance and deceptions, obstacles and stumbling blocks—and the culture and realm of heaven—a place of limitlessness and abundance, possibilities and solutions, humility and truth, stepping-stones and breakthroughs. Our problem is that the culture we grew up with will always hold us back unless we are willing to let it go to embrace the new. We are stretched, as if by wild horses, between our two worlds. If we try to straddle one foot in the finite, physical world and the other in the infinite, spiritual world, we easily become people of two minds. We can be people of carnal desires with spiritual ambitions. But one realm must have control and dictate our actions in the other. We will never have the discipline in the natural to do the impossible if we do not keep the spiritual in its proper place of precedence.

It is a simple biblical principle: those who would walk in the realm of the spirit and enter the kingdom of God must choose to be like the child (spirit) within them. (See Matthew 18:1–5.) We must choose the truths of the spirit that we are still growing into and reject the parameters set by the natural world, because until we can embrace the childlike faith that "with God all things are possible" (Matt. 19:26), we will forever be limited in what we can accomplish. In the same way, until we can overcome the weaknesses of our physical desires and needs, we will never pursue the spirit far enough to tap into the power of God.

In *With Christ in the School of Prayer*, Andrew Murray describes the process of growing into spiritual authority and competence in this way:

> The words of John (1 John 2:12–14) to little children, to young men, and to fathers, suggest the thought that there often are in the Christian life three great stages of experience....
>
> In Christ's teaching on prayer, there appear to be three stages in the prayer-life, somewhat

analogous. In the Sermon on the Mount we have the initial stage: His teaching is all comprised in one word, Father. Pray to your Father, your Father sees, hears, knows, and will reward: *how much more* than any earthly father! Only be childlike and trustful. Then comes later on something like the transition stage of conflict and conquest, in words like these: "This sort goeth not out but by fasting and prayer;" "Shall not God avenge His own elect who cry day and night unto Him?" And then we have in the parting words, a higher stage. The children have become men: they are now the Master's friends, from whom He has no secrets, to whom He says, "All things that I heard from my Father I made known unto you;" and to whom, in the oft-repeated "whatsoever ye will," He hands over the keys of the kingdom. Now the time has come for the power of prayer in His Name to be proved.[3]

How many of the people of God today are limited in this way by wisdom that comes from the world and keeps them childish and selfish instead of humbly and openly embracing the possibilities of God that allow them to grow into the fullness of maturity in Christ? There is a big difference between being childish and childlike. The first is self-absorbed, lazy, and undisciplined; the second lays down one's own wisdom and position for that which comes from above, leaning not to one's own understanding (Prov. 3:5), and is disciplined by a love that "bears all things, believes all things, hopes all things, endures all things" (1 Cor. 13:7). It's like the story of the emperor's new clothes. To be childlike is to have the simple, frank honesty of a child to realize that sometimes the doctrines we are dressing ourselves up in are nothing more than air and hubris. Instead we must earnestly seek to develop and discipline our senses in the spirit that we might become more proficient in the reality of spiritual things. This cannot be done without a prayer life that is active, unrelenting, and thriving.

GOOD THINGS OR GOD THINGS?

If we took a survey, I would bet you that far more than half of Christians would either say they believe God doesn't speak to people today as He did to the people during biblical times or that His voice comes only through tradition, the words of Scripture, or the leaders of their churches. I imagine most believers would say He rarely speaks to the common person sitting in a pew. Not only that, but there are tens of thousands of different ways in which this is taught, and thus tens of thousands of different denominations that have been formed—tens of thousands of different "day cares" housing toddlers who will never grow up because they are too attached to the earth and too disconnected from heaven. Sadly, that equals hundreds of millions of believers who will never grow up into what God has for them—and the world we live in is the worse for it.

Now I am not trying to be critical of our churches today—I'm really not. Every follower of Jesus—baby, toddler, growing adult, or elder—is my brother or sister in Christ. I am part of them as a member of the body of Christ on the earth, and if I am going to grow up in spiritual things, I need to have their welfare and blessing as much in my heart as Jesus does in His. The truth is it is likely there are things they know that I need to know to accomplish all God has called me to do. I will never really be able to accomplish my mission on the earth without them accomplishing theirs as well. Why? Because if God's will for good is not being done on the earth today, either we as Christians *as a whole* have deceived ourselves in some way that is keeping us from the power of God or else there is something we are supposed to be doing that we are not. It doesn't take an Einstein to look at the world today and come to the conclusion that God doesn't exist, He is sadistic, or for some reason things are not the way He wants them to be. Because I know that God exists and that He is good, I also know the last of these options must be true. There is some disconnect between heaven and earth, and if that divide is not on God's side, then it must be on ours.

Too many of us as Christians are ineffective in our missions because of this very disconnect. We are not plugged into the heavenly headquarters that is trying to coordinate our individual part in God's overall strategies and campaigns. Too many "generals" are doing their own thing rather than doing God's thing. Too many foot soldiers are doing little or nothing at all. Too few are getting in on the big conversation that is going on in God's throne room in which all of the shortages, deficiencies, and exploitations of the earth are being troubleshot and addressed with the wisdom of God. The answers are there, the long-term solutions are there, but there is nothing but a bunch of toddlers rolling around on the floor self-absorbed, bickering, and crying, too lost in their own worlds and shortcomings to listen in and translate God's instructions into programs of action and victory upon the earth.

Toddlers don't transform kingdoms—at least not in good ways. If we want to plug into the purposes, plans, and victory strategies of heaven, then we have to endure the rigors of the boot camp of prayer and pass its obstacle courses and challenges with flying colors.

A New Mind-Set for Prayer

While much of the religious world would have us think that God is a distant curmudgeon, stingy with His blessings and advice, that is simply not the picture Jesus painted by starting His teachings on prayer telling us to open with "our Father." As if we didn't understand from those two words, He goes on to explain, "If you, being corrupted and selfish, know what is good to give to your children, how much more does God know what is good to give you?" (See Matthew 7:11.)

It's an analogy worth taking a little further.

If God is our Father and He is good, just what kind of parent is He? Scripture tells us that He loves us, that He created everything in the universe just so we would have a place where we could live and He could walk with us, that He is not short of resources with which to bless us, and that "every good gift and every perfect gift" (James 1:17) comes from Him. However, good parents never give their children anything that they know will harm them. They don't spoil their children, nor do they pamper them or do anything that would encourage them to remain immature, selfish, and incapable of playing well with others. Good parents, like good coaches, want their children (or members of their team) to reach their full potential.

Success in life and victory on the field of competition depend on competence and excellence. Good parents don't want their kids to grow up physically but continue living in the basement because their children don't have self-discipline. They will never abandon their children, but they also want them to have lives, loves, and children of their own. God wants the same things for each of His children as well, but too many of us want to be coddled rather than disciplined.

Look for a moment at how the writer of Hebrews expresses this need to spiritually mature as God's sons and daughters:

> "My son, do not regard lightly the discipline of the Lord, nor be weary when reproved by him. For the Lord disciplines the one he loves, and chastises every son whom he receives."

It is for discipline that you have to endure. God is treating you as sons. For what son is there whom his father does not discipline? If you are left without discipline, in which all have participated, then you are illegitimate children and not sons. Besides this, we have had earthly fathers who disciplined us and we respected them. Shall we not much more be subject to the Father of spirits and live? For they disciplined us for a short time as it seemed best to them, but he disciplines us for our good, that we may share his holiness. For the moment all discipline seems painful rather than pleasant, but later it yields the peaceful fruit of righteousness to those who have been trained by it.

Therefore lift your drooping hands and strengthen your weak knees, and make straight

paths for your feet, so that what is lame may not
be put out of joint but rather be healed. Strive
for peace with everyone, and for the holiness
without which no one will see the Lord.

—Hebrews 12:5–14, esv

If we kids are going to stay "in the family business,"
we need to keep in close contact with God. We can't
just come by on Sundays for brunch; at the minimum
we should be receiving daily instructions, if not hourly.
If we are doing something truly world changing, then
we should be communicating even more frequently
than that. We should have regular planning meetings
and strategy summits with God and one another. We
should be in constant two-way communication about
every detail of what needs to be done along the way.
We should endure the times of silence in prayer as well
as the times of overflowing revelation. We should also
be partnering together in Dad's work, "joined and knit
together by what every joint supplies, according to the
effective working by which every part does its share,
caus[ing] growth of the body for the edifying of itself
in love" (Eph. 4:16). It is only when we can do this that
nothing shall be impossible for us.

Calling God "Father" demands a different type of relationship with Him. A god is worshiped and obeyed but rarely known or understood. A father is different. When we are children, we live in close union with our fathers—we live in his house, under his protection, and in his care. He is the one who gives us our weekly allowances, provides for us, and tucks us into bed at night. He talks with us and tries to answer our questions, not make life even more mysterious and obscure than it already is. He corrects us when we misstep.

As we submit to his authority and grow under it, he leads by virtue rather than demanding obedience like a dictator threatening punishment. He is no idle idol; he is a living, breathing father we touch base with every day and have access to every moment. As a loving daddy, he longs to provide our hearts' desires but will never give us something he knows will hurt us.

Now think about going to your father when you want him to give you something. The way you ask matters even more than what you want, doesn't it? Not only does a good father demand the "magic words" of *please* and *thank you*, but also if you ask casually, chances are he won't think you are serious, so he won't give you what you want right away. He will wait to see if you ask again. He wants to see if you are willing to work for it and show yourself responsible enough to handle it. If a child asks disrespectfully or selfishly, how is the father going to respond? If the child hasn't spoken with him for some time and then calls up, spits out a list of things he or she wants or needs, then abruptly hangs up, how would an earthly father respond? If even earthly fathers know that giving children something when they are disrespectful is bad for them, how much more does our heavenly Father know it?

He also does not want to give you something you cannot handle. He is not going to give a six-year-old a car, nor is he going to give a sixteen-year-old a car until that child gets a license and proves he or she can be safe on the road. Sometimes God's answer is as much in the nature of the asker as in the asking. As Spider-Man's uncle told him, "With great power comes great responsibility." Would a good father ever give great power to someone who shows no responsibility?

This is the maturing process that happens in prayer. Sometimes we ask, and in return we are asked to do something rather than receive an immediate answer. Is this a no? Not really. It is more of a "let's give it some time and we will see." After all, is there any child who has never been told by his father, "Let's wait until you are a little older before we think about that"? There are so many things God wants to give, but until we mature in the faith and in our character enough to show that we can handle these gifts, it would be irresponsible for Him to do so.

God doesn't give mixed blessings, for in Him "there is no variation or shadow of turning" (James 1:17). There is no dark side to God's gifts—there is no apparent blessing that will ultimately turn into a curse. However, if we stay in close contact with Him and on the course He sets before us, there will be nothing we can't ultimately accomplish. There is no guarantee of blessing in the disconnect, however. When we go it alone, we set our own limits on what the grace of God can do in our lives, just as the Israelites did. (See Psalm 78:41.)

Peter also speaks of this growing up process as we continually present ourselves to God in prayer: "Therefore humble yourselves under the mighty hand of God, that He may exalt you in *due time*, casting all your care upon Him, for He cares for you" (1 Pet. 5:6–7, emphasis added). When is *due time?* It is when we are mature enough for God to promote us into our next phase of responsibility and leadership authority without our childishness derailing the blessing.

Friends, it's time to grow up.

THE IMPOSSIBLE DREAM

Do you have a dream from God that people have told you is impossible to realize? If you are not getting power from God to live every day in that dream, then you are living in your own strength, not God's. If you're not actively aware of your shortcomings in accomplishing what God has put on your heart and not seeking Him daily for the wisdom and character to see it come into fruition, then what are you doing? Worldly wisdom will never right the world system. Only the wisdom and power of heaven can do that!

Prayer is the conduit to whatever we need to turn this world upside right, because it is in prayer that we become the children of God—by getting in step with the leadership of the Holy Spirit: "For as many as are led by the Spirit of God, these are sons of God" (Rom. 8:14). How do people know you are a child of God? They see evidence that you are led by His Spirit, which gives way to miraculous things that happen around you.

That is why the apostle Paul told us we needed to "pray without ceasing" (1 Thess. 5:17). You can't be led by someone you never hear from or take the time to talk with.

In his book *Just Courage*, Gary Haugen speaks of the calling and work of Mother Teresa: "Mother Teresa said that she couldn't imagine doing her work for more than thirty minutes without prayer. Do you and I have work that we can't imagine doing for thirty minutes without prayer?"[4] If we don't truly have instruction and strength from heaven for what we are doing periodically throughout the day, then who are we really working for? If we don't rely on God's abilities and wisdom every minute of every day to accomplish the tasks before us, whose strength are we operating under? Do we really think we can work without God's incredible power to overcome the problems our world faces? If it is something we can accomplish without needing to pray every thirty minutes or so, if we can in essence do it in our own strength and wisdom, are we really striving to accomplish anything that significant?

After being baptized by John, the first message Jesus preached was on what the kingdom of God is all about:

> The Spirit of the LORD is upon Me, because He has anointed Me to preach the gospel to the poor; He has sent Me to heal the brokenhearted, to proclaim liberty to the captives and recovery of sight to the blind, to set at liberty those who are oppressed; to proclaim the acceptable year of the LORD.
>
> —LUKE 4:18–19

Today poverty still cripples the vast majority of the nations of our world. There are still people who go to bed hungry every night and who have no clean water to drink. Because of this, their children are often sick, and many don't live past the age of five. Selfishness and oppressive circumstances still break families, lives, and hearts every day. Slavery and sex trafficking are more prevalent today than ever in the history of the world—and much of it involves children. Sickness, disease, and disabilities are still not a thing of the past. Murder and religious, racial, political, and economic oppression still ravage neighborhoods, nations, and continents. Then we still have friends and neighbors who don't know Jesus. Christ came to do much that still has not been done.

In John 17, which records Jesus's high priestly prayer, Christ prays that everything God made available to Him while He was on the earth would be made available to us: His glory, His power, His love. Look for a moment at the end of that prayer:

> I do not pray for these alone [the disciples], but also for those who will believe in Me through their word [that means you and me]; that they all may be one, as You, Father, are in Me, and I in You; that they also may be one in Us, that the world may believe that You sent Me. And the glory which You gave Me I have given them, that they may be one just as We are one: I in them, and You in Me; that they may be made perfect in one, and that the world may know that You have sent Me, and have loved them as You have loved Me.
>
> Father, I desire that they also whom You

gave Me may be with Me where I am, that they
may behold My glory which You have given Me;
for You loved Me before the foundation of the
world. O righteous Father! The world has not
known You, but I have known You; and these
have known that You sent Me. And I have
declared to them Your name, and will declare it,
that the love with which You loved Me may be
in them, and I in them.

—JOHN 17:20–26

In this prayer, there are further clues for us about
tapping into all God has for us through prayer. We will
discuss several of them in later chapters: that we would
be one with each other as we become one with Jesus,
that we would know His glory and power and see it
manifested upon the earth, and that we would exude His
love so that everything we set our hands to will prosper.

The bottom line is that there is no way to be an
effective Christian if you do not have a regular time of
prayer and Bible reading for at least a half hour every
day. As members of His family, we have the right to
go to our Father and ask for His plans, strategies,
and resources to fulfill our mission, assignments, and

purpose on the earth. Prayer is the conduit that not only reveals the will of God for our individual lives, but also helps make us the people we need to be to do the impossible on the earth. It's time to plug into that power like we never have before.

> Prayer itself is an art which only the Holy Ghost can teach us.... Pray for prayer—pray till you can pray.
>
> —CHARLES H. SPURGEON[5]

2

FIRST THINGS FIRST
Spirit and Truth

Hallowed be Your name.
—Matthew 6:9

Seek first the kingdom of God and His righteousness,
and all these things shall be added to you.
—Matthew 6:33

O N A SATURDAY evening in mid-November 1825, a twenty-year-old theology student named George Müller slipped into a prayer meeting in a small cottage near the school he was attending. Although he was studying to be a minister, George was not a man who lived to please God. He was a thief, a con artist, a swindler, and a heavy drinker, to name a few of his shortcomings. His father thought the ministry would provide a comfortable living for George, so he sent him off at ten years of age to begin his training, but the lack of parental guidance harmed George's character.[1]

Years later, George had little to show for his Bible training. As his mother lay on her deathbed, George sat at a card table playing until 2:00 a.m., and the next morning he went with friends to a bar that they eventually stumbled out of half-drunk. At sixteen he spent roughly a month in prison for running up a large bill at an inn and then trying to skip out without paying. Later, in order to make a trip he had always wanted to take, he pawned his schoolbooks, collected on some of his father's debts without his dad's knowledge, and headed to Switzerland with some friends for a forty-three-day romp. Because he handled their common purse, George made his friends pay roughly twice as much for the trip as he did. Though from time to time George tried to turn his life around, he was a scoundrel through and through, headed for a life of living off the graces of others—that is, if he managed to stay out of prison.

At that prayer meeting, however, George discovered something he had never experienced before. While he knew about piety and had seen the disciplined devotion of fellow students at the theological school, here he found simple, genuine faith. As the leader of the group fell to his knees—something George had neither done himself nor ever seen anyone else do—and began to pray, George couldn't help thinking, "I could not pray as well, though I am much more learned than this illiterate man."[2] The man spoke as if he knew God was actually listening.

A peace fell over the room. Standing there as the man prayed, George realized he was experiencing something he never had before—he was simply *happy*, though he had no earthly means of explaining why. In all his striving, in all his conniving to get what he wanted, in all his indulgences, it was a feeling he had never experienced. On the way home he told his friend, "All we have seen on our journey to Switzerland, and all our former pleasures, are as nothing in comparison with this evening."[3]

In the following days George returned again and again to these meetings. He felt waiting an entire week until the next Saturday would be too long. And each time he attended, he became more and more addicted to the peace he experienced there. His life began to change.

George was not changed overnight, though the change was indeed rapid. He no longer hung out with the friends he had frequented bars with; in fact, he stopped going to taverns all together, and he began telling the truth more and more often, even when it hurt. He still had missteps now and again, but because of his hunger for what he had experienced at this man's home, George was willing to give up everything he had known before. He found himself engrossed in the Scriptures, praying instead of worrying whenever an issue crossed his mind, a question occurred, or a need arose. He began attending church for the right reason, loving those around him more easily, and standing with

Christ more often, even though he still sometimes mocked the piety of his fellow students. There was no question about it: God was doing a transformational work in George Müller's heart.

In the coming years, George learned to cling to the leadership and teachings of the Holy Spirit above any other authority or personal desire. In his writings, he described his interactions with God as his life began to change:

> The Lord very graciously gave me, from the very commencement of my divine life, a measure of simplicity and of childlike disposition in spiritual things, so that whilst I was exceedingly ignorant of the Scriptures, and was still from time to time overcome even by outward sins, yet I was enabled to carry most minute matters to the Lord in prayer. And I have found "godliness profitable unto all things, having promise of the life that now is, and of that which is to come." Though very weak and ignorant, yet I had now, by the grace of God, some desire to benefit others, and he who so faithfully had once served Satan, sought now to win souls for Christ.[4]

George began spending hours each evening in prayer and reading the Bible, letting the Holy Spirit be his teacher:

> God then began to show me…that the Word of God alone is our standard of judgment in spiritual things; that it can be explained only by the Holy Spirit; and that in our day, as well as in former times, He is the teacher of His people…. The result of this was, that the first evening that I shut myself into my room, to give myself to prayer and meditation over the Scriptures, I learned more in a few hours than I had done during a period of several months previously. But the particular difference was, that I received real strength for my soul in so doing. I now began to try by the test of the Scriptures the things which I had learned and seen, and found that only those principles, which stood the test, were of real value.[5]

George's study of the Bible under the strict tutelage of the Holy Spirit over the next several years formed within him rather strict convictions about the handling of money. First of all, he felt he should rely entirely upon God for his support as a minister, so he asked that the church give him no fixed salary, only that they should pass on to him the free will offerings of any who designated that their giving go to his support. Second, he would never ask anyone for financial help when preaching or at any other time. When he needed money for something, he would go to God in prayer for it but never to any person. Third, he would always spend any money entrusted to him either on his needs, in support of the poor, or for the work of the kingdom as the demand came. He would keep no savings in the bank, but request and use money as he needed it. And last, he would never borrow money for any reason, either for personal use or for the work God gave him to do.

With these convictions, one would guess that he went on to be a very devout but poor minister for the rest of his life, going from speaking engagement to speaking engagement, living hand to mouth, but walking like a saint upon the earth always humble and dependent upon God for his next meal. However, in 1832 George moved from Germany to Bristol, England, where he took over as a pastor and went on to form the Scriptural Knowledge Institution. Through it he began day schools for poor children, Sunday schools, and other mission and Bible work, never asking anyone for a penny to support the work. In 1835, seeing the need of orphans to be raised in the Word of God, George spent a great deal of time in prayer about opening an orphanage. In the end, he resolved that God wanted him to do so, so part of his daily prayer burden was now to not only raise money to rent and furnish a home for orphans, but also to see to their daily care, clothing, and feeding. The first home housed thirty children, and in the coming years, three more buildings were added until the total number of orphans rose to about one hundred twenty.

There were several thin times, but the children never went without a meal.

> One morning the plates and cups and bowls on the table were empty. There was no food in the larder, and no money to buy food.
>
> The children were standing waiting for their morning meal, when Mueller said, "Children, you know we must be in time for school." Lifting his hand he said, "Dear Father, we thank Thee for what Thou art going to give us to eat."

There was a knock on the door. The baker stood there, and said, "Mr. Mueller, I couldn't sleep last night. Somehow I felt you didn't have bread for breakfast and the Lord wanted me to send you some. So I got up at 2 a.m. and baked some fresh bread, and have brought it."

Mueller thanked the man. No sooner had this transpired when there was a second knock at the door. It was the milkman. He announced that his milk cart had broken down right in front of the orphanage, and he would like to give the children his cans of fresh milk so he could empty his wagon and repair it.[6]

George continued to pray and walk out the ministry God laid upon his heart each and every day. After some time, he felt it was not right to rent houses in different areas for the children. They needed a central location that they owned themselves large enough for all of the children to live together. They would need £15,000 to build a home for 300 children, so George and his staff went to prayer. The home was opened in 1849. But again, they saw the need to help orphaned children was still unmet, so they prayed for more. In

1857 and 1862 a second and third home were added
for another 950 orphans at a cost of £35,000. Then
in 1869 and 1870 a fourth and fifth building were
added at an expense of £50,000, bringing the total
number of orphans housed to about 2,100. None
of this diminished the other work of the Scriptural
Knowledge Institution in its schools and missions or
its distribution of Bibles and tracts.

It was never easy, but then very few things worth
doing ever are. God led George Müller day by day, step
by step, and each day he was growing in faith and trust
so that believing for the daily needs of the growing
orphanages and schools was no greater than believing
for his own daily needs. He never took a step without
first resolving the issue in his heart through prayer and
knowing whatever course he was about to take was
already accomplished in the spirit. As he wrote in early
1850, shortly after the building of the first orphanage
house:

> While the prospect before me would have been
> overwhelming had I looked at it *naturally*, I
> was never, even for once, permitted to question
> what would be the end. For as, from the

beginning, I was sure *that it was the will of God* that I should go to the work of building for him this large Orphan House, so also, from the beginning, I was as certain that the whole would be finished as if the building had been already before my natural eyes, and as if the house had been already filled with three hundred destitute orphans.[7]

George Müller's life, as he attested himself, was an experiment in faith and the power of what prayer can accomplish even in the hands of one simple man. Throughout his life George gave roughly 85 percent of his salary away. The Holy Spirit's leadership of George through prayer was deliberate and systematic, and through it he learned the key to answered prayer. As he wrote of his aims in the life he chose:

The first and primary object of the work [of the Orphan Houses] was, and still is: that God *might be magnified* by the fact, that the orphans under my care are provided, with all they need, *only by prayer and faith*, without any one being asked by me or my fellow-laborers, whereby it may be seen, that God is faithful still, and hears prayers still.[8]

THE KEY TO ANSWERED PRAYER

In these words from George Müller and in the second line of the prayer Jesus teaches His disciples, we are given the litmus test of answered prayer: Is the purpose of the request to honor God? Does it magnify His name upon the earth? Are we asking selfishly for our own glory or for the glory of God?

When we pray, "Hallowed be Your name," it is an act of worship. However, even more than that, it is saying, "May every request that follows in this prayer be for Your glory and Your glory alone."

The "qualifiers" for answered prayer, which are outlined in the Scriptures, are not many. For example, look at what the following passages have to say about them:

> *Whatever* things you ask in prayer, *believing*, you will receive.
> —MATTHEW 21:22, EMPHASIS ADDED

Therefore I say to you, *whatever* things you ask when you pray, *believe* that you receive them, and you will have them.

—MARK 11:24, EMPHASIS ADDED

Whatever you ask *in My name*, that I will do, that *the Father may be glorified* in the Son.

—JOHN 14:13, EMPHASIS ADDED

If *you abide in Me*, and *My words abide in you*, you will ask what you desire, and it shall be done for you.

—JOHN 15:7, EMPHASIS ADDED

And in that day you will ask Me nothing. Most assuredly, I say to you, *whatever you ask the Father in My name He will give you*. Until now you have asked nothing in My name. Ask, and you will receive, that your joy may be full.

—JOHN 16:23–24, EMPHASIS ADDED

For all the promises of God in Him are Yes, and in Him Amen, *to the glory of God through us*.

—2 CORINTHIANS 1:20, EMPHASIS ADDED

If any of you lacks wisdom, let him *ask of God*, who gives to all liberally and without reproach, and it will be given to him.

—James 1:5, emphasis added

You do not have because *you do not ask*. You ask and do not receive, because *you ask amiss*, that you may spend it on your pleasures.

—James 4:2–3, emphasis added

Now this is the confidence that we have in Him, that if we ask anything *according to His will*, He hears us. And if we know that He hears us, whatever we ask, we know that we have the petitions that we have asked of Him.

—1 John 5:14–15, emphasis added

These are the promises for answered prayer in a nutshell. When you look at them all together, there isn't much room for misunderstanding what Jesus wanted us to know about the requirements for effective prayer. We can ask "whatever" we want, and we will receive what we seek, if we ask "believing," "in Jesus's name," "abiding in Him," "His Word abiding in us," "according to His will"; if we "ask not amiss," "not that we may spend it on our own pleasures and lusts," but "for the glory of God." Simple enough, don't you think?

The Bible is very clear in these verses about God's end of the equation. All of the qualifications are on our end. Let me say that another way: *If there is a problem with our prayers being answered, it is on our end, not on God's.* There is nothing wrong with God's broadcast signal, but unless we are tuned in correctly, we are not going to receive it. If you have been wondering why your prayers remain unanswered, here is your answer. You are failing in one of the areas above. You need to persevere until you have correctly dialed into God's frequency of answers.

A lot of religious teaching has muddied these waters, however, and I want to deal with the major objections I hear all the time. But first I want you to understand that the attitude George Müller and centuries of others had when they came to God in prayer is key. *Prayer is answered only when its ultimate motive is the magnification and glorification of God.*

Worship, Worship, Worship

I love the opportunity to visit different churches each week and hear the various styles of praise and worship that are offered to the Lord. I truly believe breakthroughs are made in the spirit as we lift our voices and our hands to God showing Him we are not ashamed to shout His name and stand up for Him upon the earth. But worship only *begins* when the church gathers together to praise His name. If we don't take our worship from the church into the streets and to where we live, our worlds are never going to change. Until we live our worship of God every minute of every day of every week, we are just playacting.

I don't mean we should be singing and raising our hands at work, shouting about the greatness of God. What I do mean is that living a life of integrity and honor where we work, where we live, and where we play is the backbone of spreading God's kingdom on the earth. It is worship in action. Neither is it something that you can do without the strength found in prayer.

Every act of integrity during the workweek, every step along the extra mile, every impression of excellence we leave on those around us is also worship, whether it be through volunteering, working at our jobs, or putting food on the table for our families. It is turning off the television and engaging with our spouses and children. It's checking in, not checking out. It is being every inch of who God has called us to be. It is being a shining beacon of God's goodness in our communities—the light shining on the hilltop that cannot be hidden. It is being a good steward of our resources as well as maximizing our talents. It is always growing and being teachable. It is standing up for what is right in a loving way. It is putting God first in everything and seeking His guidance in every endeavor before we do anything else.

Worship is the foundational attitude of all effective prayer. For this reason, it is the first petition of the prayer that Jesus taught.

Perhaps that is why new Christians are so effective and effervescent in their prayer lives and Christian walks while some of us who have been in the faith longer have begun to lose our enthusiasm. Jesus hasn't changed, God hasn't changed, and certainly the Word hasn't changed, but somehow through the years we become less plugged in than we used to be. Our first love has waned. The fact is, we tend to simply get distracted with the business of life, or as Jesus put it, "the cares of this world, the deceitfulness of riches, and the desires for other things" (Mark 4:19).

Rarely is it the big things that pull us away from God, but rather the small decisions. Slipping away from God usually starts when we start to skip our regular prayer times. We get up a little late and have to get to work a little early, so we think, "Oh, well, I'll just spend some time in prayer tonight." Then that night we stay up late helping one of our kids with homework, so we say, "I'll just do it in the morning." It could be any number of really important things you need to do. Jesus was not saying that the cares of this world—caring for your family, paying your rent, going to school or a job, working on your car, or any of a hundred other things—are bad. He was saying that *we can't afford to let them get in the way of getting our daily instructions from heaven's headquarters!*

The Bible says you should live "casting all your care upon Him, for He cares for you" (1 Pet. 5:7). God doesn't want you to neglect your cares; He wants to help you take care of them. He wants to give you wisdom about how to handle them—whether it is a relationship, a project at work, volunteering at your kids' school, or your passion to see a world issue resolved justly. He wants to give you strength to handle it. He has the wisdom you need to make it right. He wants to see you succeed so that He can be glorified in you.

You may read about someone like George Müller and think we are all supposed to be like him—forsaking all and depending on prayer and faith for every meal—but look at what George himself said about people who work in companies or own businesses. Prayer is not separated from what we do in the world; rather, it should be at the center of our lives whether we make a salary or pay salaries. We should have the same faith to operate a business as Müller did to run orphanages.

> Brethren in business...suffered in their souls, and [bring] guilt on their consciences, by carrying on their business almost in the same way as unconverted persons do. The competition in trade, the bad times, the over-peopled country, were given as reasons why, if the business were carried on simply according to

the word of God, it could not be expected to do well. Such a brother, perhaps, would express the wish that he might be differently situated, but very rarely did I see *that there was a stand made for God, that there was the holy determination to trust in the living God, and to depend on Him, in order that a good conscience might be maintained.* To this class, likewise, I desired to show by a visible proof, that God is unchangeably the same.[9]

George Müller understood the pressures of business and working in a secular workplace, and he acknowledged that not everyone was called to live as he did. Yet no matter what we do, we are to do it for the glorification of God, depending wholeheartedly upon Him.

If you are called to work in a secular job or run your own business, then you should be relying on God, through prayer and faith, to infuse you with His wisdom and power so that you will reflect Him in your workplace or marketplace. Just as there are those like George Müller who depend only on God for their needs, there must be people like the baker in the story

I shared earlier who are sensitive enough to the Spirit of God to hear the need in their heart and be willing to get up at 2:00 a.m. to see that God's children are provided for.

You see, Paul's admonishment to "pray without ceasing" (1 Thess. 5:17) was not just for ministers. He literally meant that there is a way to plug into the big conversation throughout the day no matter what we are doing. The reason for this is that prayer is not so much the practice of folding your hands, closing your eyes, and kneeling at the foot of your bed or in a pew as it is an attitude of constantly listening for God's instructions as you go through the day. Brother Lawrence called this "practicing the presence of God." As he put it, "There is not in the world a kind of life more sweet and delightful than that of a continual conversation with God: those only can comprehend it who practice and experience it."[10]

What is the key to maintaining this "continual conversation"? Maintaining the attitude of worship in every step of your day. This is to "walk in the Spirit" (Gal. 5:25). While most of us know we are to "pray without ceasing" (1 Thess. 5:17), that is only part of the instruction Paul was giving. I really believe what surrounds that phrase is the key to maintaining such a constant awareness that translates into unending prayer:

> Rejoice always, pray without ceasing, in everything give thanks; for this is the will of God in Christ Jesus for you.
> —1 Thessalonians 5:16–18

Being in a continual attitude of rejoicing is the entrance into prayer. Being grateful and filled with thanksgiving is how we come out of it. Then the cycle repeats itself—immediately.

How we worship God, how excellently we live to reflect His glory back to Him every day of our lives, is our boot camp of faith, our training ground for the mission and assignment He has for us. When someone is in boot camp he learns to shine his shoes, keep his bunk immaculate, and show respect to every other soldier around him. It is also where he is tested. In boot camp, recruits are presented with obstacles and told to overcome them. If they do, they are presented with bigger obstacles; if they don't, they are sent back to the end of the line to start over again.

As God recruits us and begins to work within us for our growth, we face a similar series of obstacle courses to overcome in prayer. Will we faithfully endure to see things manifested, or will we give up early? Will we put others before ourselves, or will we cave in to the lie that if we don't look out for ourselves, no one will? How we respond to these situations will show us how large an assignment God can trust us with. The beginning of effective prayer is learning to continually walk in worship, with our main goal always being to increase and experience the glory of God. Without it, we can do nothing; with it, nothing is beyond our doing.

> The end we ought to propose to ourselves is to become, in this life, the most perfect worshippers of God we can possibly be, as we will be through all eternity.
> —Brother Lawrence[11]

3

WHAT SHOULD BE
The View From the Throne Room

Your kingdom come.
—Matthew 6:10

*For the things which are seen are temporary, but
the things which are not seen are eternal.*
—2 Corinthians 4:18

We walk by faith, not by sight.
—2 Corinthians 5:7

WHAT HAPPENS WHEN we pray? Have you ever really thought about that? When you bow your knee and fold your hands or walk the floor with your eyes closed, opening your heart to heaven, what exactly happens?

There are very few references in the Bible about the proper procedures for how to pray, and I believe that is because prayer is more about the heart's attitude and focus than it is about whether we stand, sit, close our eyes, or any other practice we normally associate with prayer. The truth be told, if we are supposed to pray without ceasing, we should also be able to work on an engine, write an e-mail, give a presentation, change a diaper, write a report, have coffee with a friend, encourage a coworker, pay our bills, and any of the other myriad of things we do in a day while still keeping the communication lines open with heaven.

I believe that every day we need focused times of prayer, but at all other times we should be in an attitude of prayer with our spiritual ears open to the thoughts of heaven. There should be seasons of intense, concentrated prayer and fasting with specified hours set aside for intercession, and there should be times when prayer is simply a regular part of our daily routine.

A great interest has arisen in the last decade around 24-7 prayer rooms where different church members pray in hour-long blocks so that unbroken intercession is raised up for their city and our world. Other churches dedicate evenings solely to prayer and worship and gather believers to lift their voices in song and petition to the Lord.

While all of these are wonderful things to do, at its essence prayer is simply conversation with God. Because we have changed passports from the kingdom of this world to the kingdom of heaven, we are members of God's family and therefore have the right to talk with our Father anytime we want because He is not limited by time and space. Yet while it isn't difficult to speak to Him, even as a babe in faith, it does take some maturity to discern His voice from the voice of our own thoughts, dreams, and desires. This is why, when I speak about prayer, I get more questions about hearing the voice of God than anything else.

How God Speaks to Us

Jesus told us, "He calls his own sheep by name and leads them out. And when he brings out his own sheep, he goes before them; and the sheep follow him, for they know his voice. Yet they will by no means follow a stranger, but will flee from him, for they do not know the voice of strangers....I am the good shepherd. The good shepherd gives His life for the sheep" (John 10:3–5, 11).

It is interesting that of all the titles Jesus could have chosen for Himself—king, high priest, revolutionary, prophet, deliverer—He chose to call Himself a shepherd and refer to His followers as sheep. Not a very world-shattering picture, is it? I am sure none of the disciples were hoping He would choose that title. I doubt they ever imagined themselves triumphantly marching into Jerusalem as a conquering flock of sheep. Once again He was setting a man-made objective and aspiration firmly on its head.

However, in this passage, Jesus also gives us a key to how we hear His voice. In the same way a flock of sheep comes to distinguish the voice of their shepherd from all the other voices, so we come to know our Father's voice. This is also the same way we come to know the voice of our parents. I remember that when I was a young girl, sometimes my family would go into a crowded place—to a busy parade or a marketplace. If I ever got separated from my mother, I knew I had only to call to her, and she would be able to pick my voice out of all the others in the crowd. And when she answered, I would immediately know her voice. Then all I would have to do was follow it until I found her.

God speaks to us in many ways, and we come to recognize His voice from all the others in the world by spending time with Him just as sheep do with their shepherd and children do with their parents. It is a matter of just being together, getting used to each other, and listening. It is not about quality time, though quality time with God is among the things I long for the most in this world, but it's about the practice of daily, consistent prayer. It is about getting up, getting dressed, and eating breakfast together, every day. It is about coming home, talking about your day, and sitting down at the dinner table together, every day. God controls the quality times when He really wants to bless us, but we control the quantity of time we sit at His feet. I know of no one who has ever had influence with God in prayer who has not spent at least one night with God as Jacob did, wrestling for His blessing. (See Genesis 32:22–32.)

I tell new Christians that they should spend at least an hour of focused time a day reading their Bibles and praying. If that is tough, break it up into a half hour in the morning and another thirty minutes in the evening, then give that time room to grow as the Holy Spirit leads. The reason Bible reading should be part of this is that the Bible is made up of sixty-six personal love letters written to you by God Himself. It is the first place we should go to learn God's style of speaking. Nothing that He says to an individual heart will ever contradict what He says to us in the Bible.

Just as you might read several books by the same author in school to become familiar with his "voice," so the Bible is a great place to start learning the way God speaks to us. And I don't mean that you should get comfortable with King James English; I mean to get so familiar with God's character through His Word that, as we might with a close friend or spouse, we know instantly whether or not something we hear is something He would say. God is not going to, for instance, ask us to do something that appeals to our selfish ambitions or that contradicts something else He already told us. He is not going to use conniving arguments or ask you to disregard the good of others to profit yourself.

We are taught about the importance of knowing the Scriptures as a means of discerning God's voice in the book of Hebrews:

> For the word of God is living and powerful, and sharper than any two-edged sword, piercing even to the division of soul and spirit, and of joints and marrow, and is a discerner of the thoughts and intents of the heart.
>
> —HEBREWS 4:12

Familiarity with the Word of God is more than memorizing scriptures. The more time we spend reading the Bible, the more it permeates our beings and clarifies the voices within us. Many confuse things and divide the world of our existence into the interior and the exterior. These are the people who would say that the spirit and the soul are the same thing, but that is not true. Like the Trinity—God the Father, the Son, and the Holy Spirit—each of us is also three parts— soul, body, and spirit. How can you tell the difference between the thoughts of your own soul, which come from your mind, will, or emotions; your physical desires, hungers, and urges; and the communications of your spirit, which have ears in the spiritual realm? When a thought comes to mind, where is it coming from— God, evil, your physical urges, or your own psyche? The answer to discerning the difference between these "voices in our heads" is learned through practice and repetition, with the Bible as your personal trainer. It is the mirror into which we look and learn who we truly are. (See James 1:23–25.)

Just because something is supernatural does not mean it is instantaneous. The baby who was born in a moment spent nine months in the womb developing from two seeds before he emerged. As Warren Buffett has said, "You can't produce a baby in one month by getting nine women pregnant."[1] Though growth is unlikely to be the same in the spirit and in the natural, every endeavor still takes time. People spend years working to become what we think were overnight successes; the fact that we hadn't heard of them before doesn't mean they just appeared out of nowhere.

The same is true with things of the spirit. There are often months, if not years, of things being cultivated in prayer before they happen "overnight" in the natural. A farmer may reap the harvest in a week, but he first had to devote months to planting, weeding, and cultivating or the crop would never have been as large or as healthy. Planting and cultivating, tilling the soil and preparing it for the next season are all hard work. So, oftentimes, is prayer.

A PLACE TO START

If you don't know how or what to pray, start with the disciple's prayer found in Matthew 6:9–13 and Luke 11:2–4. As you say each line, stop and meditate on it and pray over those things that come to mind. Visualize what the kingdom of God would look like in the lives of the people you are praying for and in your own life. As you read your Bible, note the promises and affirmations God gives concerning your life. Note the instructions for how to walk more closely with Him and what it really means to abide in Him.

You also need to find a church that welcomes the presence of God and knows how to perceive it. Discerning the presence of God is typically the first step down the path to knowing the voice of God. Praise and worship usher us into His courtyard; it is a first, vital step toward understanding what it means to enter the holy of holies on our own—to enter into the intimacy of time spent with our Daddy. There is truly no more important place on the earth that we should be. Nothing we do can substitute for being with God one-on-one.

Pete Greig of 24-7 Prayer International once said it this way:

> If the things that get born out of our prayer rooms—mission, justice, caring for the poor—if the stuff that gets born out of our prayer rooms becomes more interesting and more exciting and more important to us than the intimacy that gave birth to them—the prayer—than we have lost the heart that Jesus calls us to, which is to Himself.

We must keep recycling back into prayer, otherwise we will be a one-hit wonder, where there was an explosion of prayer, the prayer inevitably was fruitful, because intimacy often does conceive new life, and all sorts of children got born, but there was only ever one cycle. But if we want to keep moving with God then we must keep recycling ourselves into the place of intimacy and prayer with God.

We are called to be something before we do anything....It's not what we do, but it is who we are. We were chosen to be friends; we have been called to be friends of Jesus.[2]

I love this picture portraying the primary place of prayer. More than anything else, God desires our presence with Him—for us to come to the Father just to be with Him, sit in His lap, and speak with Him, which He rewards with His presence. As the Scripture says, "Draw near to God and He will draw near to you" (James 4:8).

Through the Middle Ages until the dawn of the Great Awakening, many who emphasized prayer as a chief means to knowing God were called "mystics" because people considered their openness to hearing from God and entering into His presence to be mystical pursuits. St. John of the Cross wrote of such experiences in a poem similar to the Song of Solomon called *Dark Night of the Soul*. In it he described his longing for God's presence—often through times when he felt totally rejected and abandoned by God.

The goal of prayer for these mystics was not so much to receive answers to their petitions as to immerse themselves in the person of Christ and God's great love. For them, the ultimate goal of human existence was communion with God. Some of these mystics, such as Madame Jeanne Guyon, were ardently studied by John Wesley, who was at the center of the First Great Awakening in the eighteenth century. This revival was really the beginning of the evangelical movement, a shift toward a more personal experience with God that has now spanned into four centuries.

When she was only fifteen, Jeanne Marie Bouvier de la Motte was betrothed to Jacques Guyon. Her world was the courtly finery and indiscretions of the rich in the mid-seventeenth-century France of Louis the Fourteenth. Jacques Guyon doted on his young bride when he was at home, but this was seldom. Left in virtual solitude much of the time in a huge home as her husband saw to his business, Jeanne called out to God, but she found little solace even in Him. Pregnant with her second child at the age of eighteen, Jeanne was visited by a young priest at the request of her father, thinking the man could give her the guidance she needed.[3]

The young priest, who had spent the last several years in a monastery shut away from the world, was uncomfortable in the presence of the pretty young Madame Guyon and the extravagance of the sitting room where they met. Because of this, when she told him about her hunger for God and frustration in seeking Him, he told her simply, "It is, Madame, because you seek without what you have within. Accustom yourself to seek God in your heart, and you will there find Him."[4] Then he left as fast as he could make a polite exit.

The advice proved transformational as Jeanne gave herself over to seeking God hour after hour in prayer. As she sought God, she found a faith so revolutionary she frightened the Catholic Church into trying to get rid of her. First they tried putting her away in a nunnery (her husband died when she was only twenty-six years old), hoping to stop her from teaching about prayer. They asked that she forfeit the wealth her husband had left to her and become one of the sisters. Her books and writings were banned. She did everything they asked of her, but then revival broke out at the nunnery, forcing the church to move her elsewhere for fear of another Reformation. When she settled into another nunnery, revival broke out again, and finally Jeanne was locked up in the legendary Bastille until she promised to no longer teach on prayer.

In her book *Spiritual Torrents*, an extended metaphor for the journey of prayer from one plateau of knowing God to the next, she wrote:

> As soon as a soul is brought under divine influence, and its return to God is true and sincere...God imparts to it a certain instinct to return to Him in a most complete manner, and to become united to Him. The soul feels then that it was not created for the amusements and trifles of the world, *but that it has a centre and an end*, to which it must be its aim to return,

and out of which it can never find true repose (emphasis added).[5]

I believe the *center* and *end* spoken of here is something many Christians have lost sight of today. We have become obsessed with our *ends*—the goals and dreams God gives us in our hearts—but forget about our *center*—our foundation in Christ that is the strength and source of wisdom that makes those goals and dreams possible. If we do not cling to the *center* and do everything assigned to us *from the center*, what does it really matter? If we are doing it in our own strength rather than through His (from the center), is what we are doing really from Him? Or is it just to look better to others or ease our consciences? Are we choosing to pursue our purpose more than we pursue God Himself?

God doesn't ask us to pray so that He will know what needs to be done on the earth. Twice in the Sermon on the Mount, Jesus tells us, "For your Father knows the things you have need of before you ask Him." (See Matthew 6:8, 32.) Jesus does this right before He gives the outline of the disciple's prayer, and then again right before He tells us, "But seek first the kingdom of God and His righteousness, and all these things shall be added to you" (Matt. 6:33). God doesn't need us to ask so that He will know what we want. He knows those needs already, so why does He require us to ask?

I believe God instructs us to come to Him with our petitions so that He can *infuse* us with the answers. He needs us to focus on the need or desire so that He can put into us the blessings and gifts that will draw the answer into existence. That, and I believe God wants us to spend time with Him so His relationship with us will grow. Dad wants His kids to come visit and bring the grandkids. He wants to "reason together" (Isa. 1:18) with us so that we can become emissaries of His answers. When we go to Him in prayer, He wants us to leave rejoicing, knowing our petitions have been heard and allocated for, and that we have changed through the process of receiving His response. We can be assured that help is on the way because the answer has already manifested inside of us. It is just a matter of God allowing it to be birthed into the natural, physical plane of existence.

One of the ways I think of prayer is as the act of

calling out to heaven for a lifeline. As we hold firmly to one end if it, keeping it taut, God can use it to slide down the answers to our petitions. When He throws out that line, we grab it in prayer, but if we let go of it before the answer is manifested, we become disconnected from the source of our salvation. Because of this, it is also important to let what you pray govern what comes out of your mouth. Have you ever prayed something in faith only to hear yourself an hour or so later talking about how impossible the thing is that you are believing for? How unlikely it is to happen? That is a sign that the answer has not been downloaded into your spirit and that it's time to get back to prayer on that issue. There's only one place to talk out our petitions, and it is not in front of people!

LETTING PRAYER HELP YOU SEE MORE CLEARLY

Prayer is the most powerful place of spiritual growth. Sitting in church under good teaching is a wonderful thing, and applying the principles learned there is life transforming, but your pastor can't get to know God for you. You have to take Jesus up on His invitation to come hang out. You have to spend time with your physical eyes closed and your spiritual eyes open, letting Jesus show you what He really wants for you and the plans He has for you to impact your world. It is in this place of intimacy that He hands us the keys to His kingdom.

God's kingdom is the vision of what things on this earth should really look like. Our world needs transformational Christian leadership like never before. Modern slavery and poverty need to be addressed with God's revolutionary ideas. The world's business as usual—corruption, exploitation, lack in one area while there is gross overconsumption in others—is not God's way of doing things. Why is more money spent finding out about the immorality of the rich and famous than providing children with clean water or educating those orphaned by war or AIDS? Where is our uncompromising influence for good? Where is our unquenchable thirst that God should be glorified in everything we do?

Brothers and sisters, it's time we plugged into the things of the Spirit and got serious about doing the impossible.

Pray to die to thy [physical] hearing. Then thou will rise in the [spiritual] hearing of thy Savior and then thou will hear His voice, and know it from all others. And you will be able to always obey. Pray to die to your seeing and to rise in the seeing of thy Savior, and then thou will see the difference between God's holy will, and thy carnal will. Pray to die to thy smell, and then thou will rise in the smelling of thy blessed Savior. And then thou will smell the odor of Holiness and the sweetness of His kingdom.... Pray to die to thy taste and to rise to the taste of thy Savior, which is to do all His will in all things, which is the food of thy soul, as it was the food of His soul to do His Father's will when He was on the earth.

—Rebecca Cox Jackson[6]

MISSION: ~~IMPOSSIBLE~~

Today's Place in Eternity

Your will be done on earth as it is in heaven.
—MATTHEW 6:10

Then the King will say to those on His right hand,
"Come, you blessed of My Father, inherit the kingdom
prepared for you from the foundation of the world:
for I was hungry and you gave Me food; I was thirsty
and you gave Me drink; I was a stranger and you took
Me in; I was naked and you clothed Me; I was sick
and you visited Me; I was in prison and you came to
Me....Assuredly, I say to you, inasmuch as you did it to
one of the least of these My brethren, you did it to Me."
—MATTHEW 25:34–36, 40

D O YOU WANT to be like Jesus? Really? Then let me ask you a question. What is Jesus doing right now?

That's right. He's at the right hand of the Father *praying*—interceding for us and our world (Rom. 8:27). You want to be like Jesus? Then you need to be in prayer. What is the best thing to pray? Find out what Jesus is praying at the right hand of the Father and pray in agreement with Him. Let the Jesus in you pray. Find out what Jesus thinks about matters, and let Him put the words into your mouth to pray. Is there any better person to agree with in prayer than Jesus Himself?

After you have prayed and heard in the big conversation what God's will is, then go out and be part of the manifestation of the word He has given you. Live as an answer to prayer. Live as a citizen and ambassador of the heavenly kingdom.

Before He went to the Garden of Gethsemane, Jesus paused to pray for His disciples and for us in the high priestly prayer of John 17. In this prayer, He made eight different requests on our behalf—on behalf of His disciples and those who would believe after hearing their word (that is you and me). He prayed that:

1. Jesus would be glorified so all could have eternal life (John 17:1–2, 5).

2. We would know the Father (John 17:3).

3. We would be one with one another as He is one with His Father (John 17:11, 21–23).

4. We would have His joy (John 17:13).

5. Evil would not overcome us (John 17:15).

6. Truth would separate us as His holy followers (John 17:17, 19).

7. We would see His glory (John 17:24).

8. The love God has for His Son would be in us (John 17:26).

It isn't difficult to look at Jesus's followers on the earth today and see that these prayers are largely going unanswered. There is more confusion about who God is and more denominations and schisms in the church than ever before. Divorce and depression, among other things, are destroying Christians as much as they are anyone else in the world. The essence of truth is still widely debated, God's glory isn't evident in either His church or His followers, and God's love doesn't seem to overflow to the brother or sister sitting next to us in the church pew let alone to others around the world. Is it possible that Jesus could pray for something and it not happen?

When Jesus prayed this prayer with His disciples, He wasn't just praying. He also was passing the baton to them and those who would believe in Him in the generations to come. It is one thing for Jesus to pray, but quite another for us to come into agreement with that prayer and take up His desires for our generation as if they were our own. Will we be part of the answer to Jesus's prayer or part of the problem by preventing His petitions from coming into reality? Will we pray His kingdom into the earth, or be swept away in the river of worldly culture, the busyness of life, and the mass consumerism that is distracting so many from life in the Spirit?

A Life Spent to See God's Kingdom Expanded on the Earth

I don't know whether you have seen the 2006 movie *Amazing Grace*, but it outlines the story of William Wilberforce and those who came to be known as the Clapham Sect. This group of devoted believers worked for more than four decades (from 1788 until 1833) to end slavery in the British Commonwealth and make social improvements for all classes throughout the United Kingdom. However, *Amazing Grace* tells only part of this story. What happened in the halls of Battersea Rise, the house on Clapham Common that served as the gathering place of Wilberforce and his conspirators, is a study in the role prayer plays in accomplishing what no one in Wilberforce's day thought possible.

William Wilberforce was not a man you would have picked out of a crowd as a leader or someone to admire. He was barely five feet tall, was sickly, and had weak eyes. He was virtually orphaned at only nine years old when his father died and he was sent away from his mother to live with relatives. Living with his aunt and uncle, he came under the influence of John Newton, the minister who wrote the song "Amazing Grace." Once captain of a slave vessel, Newton came to God with an incredible burden of guilt for the things he had seen and done while at sea profiting from the slave trade. Newton and the grace he wrote about were powerful influences on Wilberforce all the days of his life.[1]

Wilberforce's grandfather died when he was about sixteen, and William inherited enough money from him to live very comfortably for the rest of his life. Rather than doing that, however, young Wilberforce used his wealth and influence to win a seat in Parliament in 1780 when he was only twenty-one. He carried the conviction that "God Almighty has set before me two great objects, the suppression of the slave trade and the reformation of manners [moral values]."[2] This was no easy task, as London was veritably one vast casino at the time preoccupied with its games of chance and pursuit of pleasure.

Much of the wealth that was being gambled around was made from the labor of African slaves in the West Indies, and the poor in England were virtually sentenced to hard labor just to survive because of the work standards of the day. Men, women, and children alike were working sixteen to eighteen hours a day for a subsistence existence. Then even that was too often spent on gin to take the edge off of life rather than used to build toward a better future. It wasn't uncommon for a notorious highway robber to be hung next to a child who had stolen a loaf of bread for his siblings. William Wilberforce was determined that such things should not exist in a Christian society.

Every year from 1788 until 1791, William introduced bills calling for the abolition of slavery to the House of Commons only to see them ignored or defeated. In 1792, in the hope of being more effective in his life's mission by living closer to Parliament, William moved into the family home of friend and relative Henry Thornton. Battersea Rise was located in the township of Clapham, and within a short time the house became the gathering place of like-minded supporters of abolition and social reform. As Wilberforce presented legislation calling for freedom for all slaves almost every year from 1792 until 1804, Battersea Rise became a place of prayer, research, strategizing, and debate. Through the years Thornton added thirty-four more bedrooms to house those who came to support the work, and a library designed by Prime Minister William Pitt as a common room for their gatherings and work. Those living in Battersea Rise spent their days and nights searching records, verifying testimonies, and gathering as much evidence as possible to be presented to Parliament, hoping to sway opinions against the slave trade by exposing its barbarity. For all of this, they were scoffed at and ridiculed. According to former Member of Parliament and author Jonathan Aitken:

> For the first twenty years of his [Wilberforce's] Parliamentary struggles he suffered nothing but defeats, insults, rejection from his friends, vilification from his enemies, and even threats to his life. In the history of British politics there has been no comparable display of moral courage over such a prolonged period by a single campaigner. Perhaps Winston Churchill's lonely opposition to the appeasement of Hitler's Germany in the 1930s comes close, but his wilderness years were shorter than those endured by Wilberforce and were thwarted by fewer defeats.[3]

I want you to pause for a moment and imagine what this campaign must have been like. First of all, Wilberforce was wealthy enough to never need to work a day in his life. There was no reason except the conviction that God had put into his heart that he should ever have to do anything but enjoy life. Yet instead he chose to align himself with those considered the lowest of the low in society—African slaves—and withstand the ridicule and degradation of an entire society whose wealth was built upon the back of the very institution he was fighting to eliminate.

The meetings at Clapham were not once-a-week prayer meetings to lift up Brother So-and-so who just lost his job or to pray, "Lord, please heal Sister Johnson, if it be Your will." Clapham was a gathering place of those with the moral courage to stand against their culture for the sake of fighting prejudice, racism, corruption, and oppression. And this wasn't just a few years of work. Slavery wasn't outlawed in the British Isles until 1807—roughly two decades after the Clapham group started—and it took another twenty-five more years for slavery to be abolished in all of the British Empire, from the Yukon territory in Canada to the islands of New Zealand. In fact, the fight took literally the entirety of Wilberforce's adult life, as he died just months after the abolition of slavery in the British Empire passed in 1833.

The Clapham group's only concern was not slavery, either. Clapham frequenters founded such organizations as the Religious Tract Society, the British and Foreign Bible Society, and the Church Missionary Society, which sent missionaries to Africa, India, China, Japan, Palestine, and the nations now known as Sri Lanka and Iran. The group called for the ending of the national lottery, which was seen as a "national sin" that robbed the poor of what little money they had. Other members were directors of the Sierra Leone Company that sought to free slaves and return as many as possible to their native Africa. There also was the Society for Bettering the Condition of the Poor, the Society for the Relief of Debtors, and the Society for the Education of Africans, among others. As author Clifford Hill wrote of the Clapham group:

> Their political activity as well as their work
> outside Parliament was influential in changing

the moral values of the nation, reducing the crime rate, stabilising family life, reducing illegitimacy, drunkenness and violence, as well as in tackling poverty and improving social conditions for the poor.[4]

Francis Place, who was no friend to the Clapham group or their evangelical Christianity, wrote in 1829:

I am certain I risk nothing when I assert that more good has been done to the people in the last thirty years than in the three preceding centuries; that during this period they have become wiser, better, more frugal, more honest, more respectable, more virtuous than they ever were before.

For this transformation [John] Wesley was partly responsible, and Wilberforce and his friends built on Wesley's foundations, bringing their influence to bear in circles which the Methodists could never hope to reach.[5]

What Will You Take into Eternity?

Prayer was at the center of the Clapham group's vision and resolve. Without daily prayer to strengthen them, how could they have stayed true to their calling to end slavery in the British Commonwealth and work for the betterment of every member of British society? How could they have devised plans that would succeed without the wisdom of God? The United States' debate over the issue ended in a bloody civil war, but England experienced the transition without revolt. How could such a thing be done without the power of God being brought into the matter through daily and hourly prayer?

When we get to "Your will be done on earth as it is in heaven," in Jesus's outline of daily prayer, I believe this is the place where our hearts first turn to intercession, or praying for others. Paul described this as a "first of all" practice to take care of before we began to pray about the various concerns for our own lives.

> Therefore I exhort first of all that supplications, prayers, intercessions, and giving of thanks be made for all men, for kings and all who are in authority, that we may lead a quiet and peaceable life in all godliness and reverence. For this is good and acceptable in the sight of God

our Savior, who desires all men to be saved and
to come to the knowledge of the truth.
—1 Timothy 2:1–4

In many ways, praying for others is the cornerstone of spiritual warfare. While God loves humanity, He is not One who will miss the individual trees for the forest. He loves humanity because He loves each and every individual who comprises the vast seas of people who live on the earth. God has a plan for each and every one of their lives, but He also needs those who know Him to stand in the gap for those who don't and be an advocate to heaven on their behalf. That means that first of all we lift up the leaders of our lands and our cities, calling for God to turn the hearts of our presidents or prime ministers in the same way He turns the waters of the rivers of the earth. (See Proverbs 21:1.)

Pray that they have the wisdom to govern justly and soundly, to turn the tides of war to peace, to negotiate successful treaties, to be a blessing to allies and a stumbling block to those who distort justice for their own gains. In the same way pray for your senators and representatives in Congress, governor, city and state officials, and law enforcement officers. Hold them before God daily and ask for His influence in their lives both personally and publicly so that we may "lead a quiet and peaceable life in all godliness and reverence" (1 Tim. 2:2).

Then pray for your family members and friends in need. Pray not only in times of crisis but also preemptively. Get copies of my books *Commanding Your Morning* and *Rules of Engagement* and pray the prayers and declarations in those books over those you feel called to lift up to the Father. We must be the importune neighbors who go to our Friend at midnight and ask for bread for our guests. (See Luke 11:5–8.) We are the widows who do not give the judge rest until justice is done. (See Luke 18:2–8.) Some issues we may have to pray about only once, others may take us lifetimes as they did for those who gathered at Battersea Rise, but daily we must step into the gap for others. (See Ezekiel 22:30.) Someone must be interceding on their behalf, giving heaven the right to invade earth with God's will.

According to intercessor Rees Howells, there are three things in intercession that are not found in

ordinary prayer: identification, agony, and authority.[6]
When interceding for others, we identify with their
place just as Jesus did when He became a human being
so that His life and death might tear away the barrier
between humanity and God. He understood every
temptation that is common to being human (Heb.
4:15) and stood in our place before God on the cross of
Calvary just as He still does for us at the right hand of
the Father today.

This doesn't mean that we go to the cross for them.
That needed to be done only once; Jesus has finished
the work of the cross once and for all. Yet we can allow
ourselves to be in others' shoes as we pray. We do not
pray for them as someone superior to them but as if
we were in their place, whether they are in prison, in
temptation, or in need of God's wisdom. We seek to
lift the burdens from their shoulders in prayer. As Paul
once described it, "For I could wish that I myself were
accursed from Christ for my brethren, my countrymen
according to the flesh" (Rom. 9:3).

Herein is the agony of battling in prayer as if
suffering with them through the dark valley to God's
full salvation on the other side. We call upon heaven

for them as if we ourselves were going through whatever they are experiencing. This may call for more concentrated times of prayer or even fasting as we seek to hear clearly from heaven on their behalves. We allow the Holy Spirit to make "intercession for us with groanings which cannot be uttered" (Rom. 8:26).

Then, as we persevere in this prayer, as the work of prayer finds its completion, we experience the answer: the grace and authority needed to overcome the difficulty floods like morning light into our spirits and souls. The answer comes in our hearts, and we know without a doubt that the problem is taken care of, even if that answer has not yet manifested in the natural world. This is the assurance that allowed George Müller to thank God for breakfast even though the cupboards were bare. It is a hard thing to describe until you have experienced it, but it feels as though the burden of the matter lifts and the peace of God "which surpasses all understanding" (Phil. 4:7) floods your heart and mind.

KNOWING GOD'S WILL FOR EVERY SITUATION

Spending time reading the Bible, meditating on the Scriptures, and praying saturates our consciences with the reality of the spiritual world. It attunes our spiritual senses to hear God's voice and hones our instincts to the differences between right and wrong in every matter. As we practice this and our spirits grow toward maturity "by reason of use," our senses are "exercised to discern both good and evil" (Heb. 5:14).

This isn't just for moral issues either. These directives do not change, and we must adhere to them. Yet to do only that is not the wisdom of God but a legalism that can make a person's heart harder than those of the Pharisees and Sadducees. It was this legalistic self-justification that Jesus addressed when He warned, "For you pay tithe of mint and anise and cummin, and have neglected the weightier matters of the law: justice and mercy and faith. These you ought to have done, without leaving the others undone" (Matt. 23:23).

When we think we are "good enough" because we have adhered to our own definition of righteousness, we are like someone who stands at the edge of a precipice blind to how precariously balanced he is against a fall. We cannot be led by the Word alone; we must also be led by the Holy Spirit. And that's not all. Our understanding of the Scriptures must come with the Holy Spirit as our primary teacher, not only the pastors and the ministers we hear in church or on television. The excellence of our faith and actions does not come from our own understanding, "but our sufficiency is from God…not of the letter but of the Spirit; for the letter kills, but the Spirit gives life" (2 Cor. 3:5–6).

The word *life* used here comes from the Greek word *zoe*, which means resurrection life, or the life that God gives.[7] While it is the Word of God that introduces us to this life, it is the Spirit of God who gives this life. Have you ever seen the 2010 movie *The Book of Eli?* [If you haven't, SPOILER ALERT.] In that movie, Eli (who is played by Denzel Washington) is carrying the last known Bible on an earth decimated by war. A man named Carnegie (played by Gary Oldman) rules a small, post-apocalyptic town with an iron fist because he controls the only clean water source in the area. For decades he has been searching for a copy of the Bible because he knows its power. As he sees it:

> [The Bible's] a weapon. A weapon aimed right at the hearts and minds of the weak and the desperate. It will give us control of them. If we want to rule more than one small...town, we have to have it. People will come from all over; they'll do exactly what I tell 'em if the words are from the book. It's happened before, and it'll happen again. All we need is that book.[8]

Eli, however, is led by the Spirit in a unique way to protect the book and take it west, where it will be reproduced and distributed to all. Through this leading, he also knows that Carnegie is not the one with whom to leave the book. He must fulfill his calling and continue west even if it costs him his life.

Despite the Hollywood spin and violence of this movie, the message is one worth considering. The "Book" gives life if we read it and meditate on its words every day, which is what happens for Eli. It will help us discern good from evil if we let the Spirit of God guide us and teach us. However, it will help us decide about not only the bigger issues that it spells out, but also the small, everyday decisions that make up the incremental steps that determine whether we will be successful in our endeavors or fail. Should I start my own business or go to work for someone else? Should I partner with this person or not? Is this a person I should date? Is this the church I should be attending? God, is this particular venture Your path for me or not?

As we spend time in prayer and God's Word, the peace of God inside of us becomes the "judge" or "umpire" that helps us decide the answers to our questions as we lay them before Him. As Colossians 3:15 says, "Let the peace of God rule in your hearts." According to *Strong's Concordance*, the Greek word for *rule* here means: "1) to be an umpire, 2) to decide, determine, 3) to direct, control, rule."[9] Some people call this the difference between a "check" in their spirit and sensing peace about a particular direction. The Holy Spirit's leading is not a loud, overwhelming voice within us, but often an uneasiness or discomfort with following one path (the "check," as many describe this) and a peace or feeling of confidence about moving in another. This is the subtle directing of the Holy Spirit within our human spirits, and the more sensitive and open we are to this inner prompting, the more we will see things in our life line up as God wants them to.

This is where praying, "Lord, if it be Thy will," becomes a complete cop-out. In speaking with His disciples, Jesus said:

> You are My friends if you do whatever I command you. No longer do I call you servants, for a servant does not know what his master is doing; but I have called you friends, for all things that I heard from My Father I have made known to you.
>
> —John 15:14–15

God doesn't want us to be in the dark about things. Many look at Jesus's praying "not My will, but Yours, be done" (Luke 22:42) in the Garden of Gethsemane and forget that in the one instance He prayed this prayer, it was not because He didn't know the will of God. It was because He was agreeing to do the will of God despite the pain it would cause Him. It was a prayer of consecrating Himself to the tough road ahead to the cross, not Him saying, "Lord, I don't really know

what You want in this matter, so please do whatever
You think is best."

I do not want to suggest that it is always easy to
know God's will. It takes consistent work and a good
deal of growing up spiritually, but God's will is not
unfathomable. The mysteries of God are there for us
to solve, not for us to throw up our hands at and say,
"Well, you never really know, so why worry about it?"
They are there to make the pursuit of knowing God
that much more exciting. And if being friends with
God is not impossible, then what is?

WHY PRAYER ISN'T FOR
THE FAINT OF HEART

The desire to know God and build His kingdom is
what causes people to pray hours and hours a day and
never get bored. There are things to be birthed in the
spirit that will come only after enduring labor pains
in prayer. When we pray, there is work to be done in
the spirit that will not be done if we stop. Jesus is the
cornerstone of the kingdom of God, His Word is the
foundation, and prayer is where we receive its blueprints.

That is what tapping into the big conversation is really all about.

At the same time, I don't want to put a guilt trip on you about how much time you spend in prayer. The fact that some people pray in concentrated, focused seclusion for hours a day doesn't mean God will lead every Christian to do that. The Bible doesn't give specific guidelines for how long and how often we should pray for a reason—and that is because we are to be led by the Spirit of God in prayer as in everything else in life. There may be times when you pray for hours in a day and other times when you simply say short prayers throughout the day. On some days, prayer will feel like mining though rock, and other days it will be "joy inexpressible and full of glory" (1 Pet. 1:8).

The point is we need to be dedicated to prayer, and if we have never prayed much in the past, we need to look at it with renewed emphasis. We are being ushered to it with a fresh calling. We need to learn to operate in prayer through the small, everyday realities of life so that when God calls us to address the big, once-in-a-lifetime events, we are already practiced and prepared. We won't learn to pray down miracles until we've learned to pray down our daily bread. And we won't be disciplined in the things of the Spirit until we have learned to be disciplined in the natural. As Jesus said:

> He who is faithful in what is least is faithful also in much; and he who is unjust in what is least is unjust also in much. Therefore if you have not been faithful in the unrighteous mammon [*or worldly wealth*], who will commit to your trust the true riches? And if you have not been faithful in what is another man's, who will give you what is your own?
>
> —LUKE 16:10–12

Now that we have the big picture vision of what God wants to do, it is time to get down to the nuts and bolts of day-to-day living.

> God does nothing but in answer to prayer....In souls filled with love, the desire to please God is a continual prayer. As the furious hate which the devil bears us is termed the roaring of a lion, so our vehement love may be termed crying after God.
>
> —JOHN WESLEY[10]

PART TWO

Praying Heaven Down

Give us this day our daily bread. And forgive us our debts, as we forgive our debtors. And do not lead us into temptation, but deliver us from the evil one. For Yours is the kingdom and the power and the glory forever. Amen.
—MATTHEW 6:11–13

5

ENOUGH

Plugging Into Heaven's Provision

Give us this day our daily bread.
—Matthew 6:11

Therefore do not worry about tomorrow, for
tomorrow will worry about its own things.
Sufficient for the day is its own trouble.
—Matthew 6:34

THE FIRST HALF of the disciple's prayer really has little to do with us as individuals. It is first about God and then about His kingdom. It is about vision and purpose, mission and assignment. It is about our identity in Him and our destiny as His children. Then it transitions. We go from plugging into eternity to what we will each do "this day," and the first priority of this day will always be our physical provisions: "Give us this day our daily bread."

If you want to check a person's level of commitment and spirituality, there are four areas you should examine: how they manage their daily calendar, their finances, their relationships, and their destiny. These four areas make up the difference between a truly rich life and a life that is in spiritual poverty. Are you living a life of investment or a life of consumption? Do you live each day maximizing your assets or making excuses for living beyond your means? Are you giving into the lives of others, or are you always the one in need of being comforted, advised, or helped out of a jam? Are you a giver or a receiver? Are you still waiting for that big break before you really get down to living the life you want to live, or are you enjoying each day for the challenges and successes it presents, seeing it as an opportunity to enjoy, grow, and build toward a better future?

Truth be told, we all probably do a bit of each, but I hope you realize that what you do with what you have today will do more for your destiny than waiting for some day when you have won the lottery or hit it big in some way. The truth of the matter is that waiting for a "someday when" never takes you anywhere. Everything you need to accomplish the dreams and goals in your heart is already in your hands, and only by investing it today will you have what you need to accomplish tomorrow's hopes and aspirations.

How Much Is an Hour of Your Time Worth?

Do you know what your most valuable commodity is as a human being on this earth? Some may say their car, their family, their job, or their investments, but the truth is, it is your time. No matter what you do, you will never be able to get any more time than you have right now. Whether you are the president of the United States, Donald Trump, or a homeless person, you will get only twenty-four hours in a day, seven days in a week, and fifty-two weeks in a year. Yet given that fact, how much value can you derive from each hour? Will it be minimum wage, the roughly $125 a minute that someone like Michael Jordan makes even while he sleeps, or the more than $10,000 a minute Bill Gates made when Microsoft stock was booming (which is, by the way, more than $15 million a day)? How do you go from earning what you do now to making thousands of dollars an hour for your time?

Believe it or not, at one time both Michael Jordan and Bill Gates earned no more than a high school student would today for each hour of their day. However, what they invested their time in when they were in high school, then in college, then in their twenties and thirties made all the difference in the world. As a tenth-grader, Michael Jordan tried out for the varsity basketball team at his high school, but he was cut because they said he was too short at only five feet, eleven inches. So what did Jordan do? He invested his time in practice rather than moping, and he went on to be a star on the junior varsity team. Over the summer, he grew four inches and took his work ethic into the rest of his career, becoming arguably the greatest basketball player of all time. By investing his time in what he loved, his "sweat equity" paid off. Even when he wasn't earning any money playing basketball, he was investing his best effort in every second—and that investment eventually paid off *big!*

In his book *Outliers: The Story of Success*, best-selling author Malcolm Gladwell discusses the incredible power of spending thousands of hours doing something you love or that greatly interests you. In fact, the first chapter of his book is titled "The Matthew Effect" and is based on Matthew 25:29: "For to everyone who has, more will be given, and he will have abundance; but from him who does not have, even what he has will be taken away."

The second chapter outlines what he calls "The 10,000-Hour Rule." In it Gladwell outlines how men such as Sun Microsystems founder Bill Joy, Microsoft founder Bill Gates, and Apple CEO Steve Jobs—all born about the same time at the dawn of the personal computer age—spent thousands and thousands of hours in computer labs tucked away from everyone else writing line after line of computer code, just seeing what they could get a computer to do. They were geeks without a social life, but what they invested themselves in paid off better for them than going out partying or attending sporting events would have.

Gladwell also talks about the Beatles, whose "overnight" success came after playing—and rather badly at first—hundreds of four- to eight-hour sets in Hamburg, Germany, before anyone in England had any idea who they were. Gladwell's point is that it's not just Gates's intelligence or the Beatles' talent that put them over the top, but the roughly ten thousand hours spent doing the right thing at the right time.

There are people out there who are smarter than Gates but are doing nothing today and people with a great passion for music who never play on a big stage. What's the difference? One invests thousands of hours working on what they love in the right place at the right time; the others spend that amount of time watching TV, chasing members of the opposite sex, or giving in to their addictions. The only thing our kids seem to spend ten thousand hours doing these days is playing video games, many of which are violent or have content that will do little to help them stay holy and pure before God.

The point is, the greatest value of our lives comes from what we do with our time, and the only time we really have control over is the current moment. There are no "overnight" successes, only people whose preparation met God-given opportunity. There will be amazing opportunities in our lives, but will you be ready for them? Have you spent the thousands of hours when no one else was looking making the proper preparations? Are you using your time today to invest in something worthwhile or doing barely enough to get by?

While the opportunities and favor in our lives come from the Lord, the preparation is up to us. Look at this story from 2 Kings as an example:

> Then he [Elisha] said, "Take the arrows"; so he [Joash, the king of Israel] took them. And he said to the king of Israel, "Strike the ground"; so he struck three times, and stopped. And the man of God was angry with him, and said, "You should have struck five or six times; then you would have struck Syria till you had destroyed

it! But now you will strike Syria only three times."

—2 Kings 13:18–19

By divine prophecy, an opportunity to destroy Israel's enemies was placed into King Joash's hands. Symbolically he was to strike the ground with his arrows as he planned to strike Syria. However, Joash's obedience was halfhearted. Rather than passionately cutting great gashes into the earth with his arrows until the prophet told him to stop, he poked aimlessly at the ground three times and then stopped. He had the opportunity to see his nation delivered from its enemies, but his own lazy, comfort-softened nature got in his way.

As King Solomon advised:

Do you see a man who excels in his work? He will stand before kings; he will not stand before unknown men.

—Proverbs 22:29

Every day, whether we are a student, a burger flipper in a fast-food restaurant, or the president of a Fortune

500 company, we have opportunities to excel at what we are doing—to make an investment to get better at something. We can work and give our all to improve ourselves or sit back and loaf. As it says elsewhere in Proverbs: "He who has a slack hand becomes poor, but the hand of the diligent makes rich" (Prov. 10:4), and "The hand of the diligent will rule, but the lazy man will be put to forced labor" (Prov. 12:24). The way we excel in our work is just as important as how faithfully we attend church. They are both part of our worship. Are you giving Christ your all—all the time—every day?

"My Grace Is Sufficient for You"

A friend recently gave me a book titled *The Storehouse Principle* by Al Jandl and Van Crouch. In it one of the authors asked the question: "Has your upkeep become your downfall?" It's not hard to look at the recent recession in the United States to see that it was due largely to the failure of tens of thousands to properly manage their credit. Greedy bankers tried to make a little extra money by stretching the rules of lending, and greedy borrowers allowed their reach to exceed their grasp by buying more than they could afford. We want the benefits of our wealth before we have worked to earn it, and oftentimes we are a lot like Joash. We want to prosper and live in peace, but when it comes right down to it, we are halfhearted and only scratch at the surface of our dreams without earnestly digging into them.

We are waiting for something from the outside to happen that will propel us over the top. We are waiting until we have more before we begin to tithe to our church or support a ministry God has put on our hearts. We look at what we have and say it is too little, barely enough to take care of ourselves, so we lock it away or hold it tightly against our bosoms to protect it, unwilling to be a giver or an investor of what we have. But as Paul advised the Corinthians:

> He who sows sparingly will also reap sparingly, and he who sows bountifully will also reap bountifully. So let each one give as he purposes in his heart, not grudgingly or of necessity; for God loves a cheerful giver. And God is able to make all grace abound toward you, that you, always having all sufficiency in all things, may have an abundance for every good work. As it is

written: "He has dispersed abroad, He has given
to the poor; His righteousness endures forever."
—2 CORINTHIANS 9:6–9

There is an interesting word in this passage in verse
8, the word *sufficiency*. The Greek word translated
as *sufficiency* here appears only in one other place in
Scripture, in Paul's letter to Timothy, where it is
translated differently:

Now godliness with *contentment* is great gain.
—1 TIMOTHY 6:6, EMPHASIS ADDED

The Greek word used here, αύτάρκεια, is made
up from two roots: *auto*, meaning "self," and *autarchy*,
meaning "sufficient and independent." According to
Strong's, the word means "a perfect condition of life in
which no aid or support is needed."[1] In other words,
it means you already have everything you need for the
task at hand within your possession. You are sufficient
unto yourself. It is what enabled Paul to say:

For I have learned in whatever state I am, to be
content: I know how to be abased, and I know
how to abound. Everywhere and in all things I

have learned both to be full and to be hungry,
both to abound and to suffer need. I can do all
things through Christ who strengthens me.
—PHILIPPIANS 4:11–13

No matter how much or how little Paul had, he could look at it and say, "This is enough to do what God has called me to do." No matter how much he had at the moment, Paul always had enough to give, enough to live, and enough to invest. Paul was no more faithful with much than he was faithful with little, and vice versa. He was no less faithful with little than he was with much. Everything he had belonged to God, so he was always *content* that what he had at the moment was always *sufficient* for whatever he was doing.

We need to look at what we have before us with the same confidence and trust. Each of us always has at least three things to invest: our time, our talents, and our treasure. We all have the same amount of time, and whatever we invest our time in—whether it is watching television or working to earn a degree—becomes more valuable to someone. In other words, the reason television, movies, sporting events, and video games are so profitable in our modern society is because so many people invest so much time in them. You can be either on the profitable side of that scenario or the paying side.

Your talents determine how much your time is worth, and how much treasure you have is a testament to the nature of your investments and financial wisdom. Are you self-controlled enough in your spending to keep bad debt from crippling your cash flow? Do you live hand-to-mouth, or do you have a surplus each month to save and invest in your future? As Edwin Louis Cole once advised, "We sow to the future and reap from the past."[2] Do you look at what you have now and say this is more than enough? Do you say, "With the simple things I have today, I will change the world"?

ABUNDANCE FROM A NUT

There is perhaps no better example of someone looking at what little they had, mixing it with his faith in God and prayer, and then turning it into world-changing abundance than that of George Washington Carver. Born in the final years of the Civil War as a slave, he never knew his father, and a raiding party kidnapped his mother and him when he was a small child. George was eventually rescued by being traded for a racehorse, but he would never see his mother again.[3]

George struck out on his own in search of an education at the age of ten, about the same time he gave his life to Jesus Christ. By working to earn his own living and pay the required school fees, he was able to start attending school regularly when he was twelve. He spent as many hours working each day as he did attending school. When the recess bell sounded, he returned home to do laundry and other chores. No matter where he worked, his schoolbooks were never far as he commonly took them with him to read during breaks or when he was doing tasks that didn't require his full attention. Neither the racial discrimination of the day nor his almost total self-dependence would keep him from learning. When he faced prejudice or tough obstacles, his gentle nature and the friends he had made along the way always helped see him through.

By the time he graduated with a master's degree in 1896, Carver was widely recognized for his excellence as a student and researcher, and he received several offers to teach or conduct research at top institutions. However, his heart told him his mission was to help eliminate poverty among former slaves in the South, so he went to work at Booker T. Washington's Tuskegee Institute. Because many former slaves had been farming to survive, agriculture was one of the Tuskegee's primary fields of study, and Carver became its leading professor and researcher.

Immediately Carver began to look for ways to improve farm profitability and sustainability. He saw that the main cash crops of cotton and tobacco quickly depleted the soil of its nitrates and other nutrients, so he looked for natural fertilizers and other ways to replenish the soil and increase the productivity of these farms. He soon found that planting peanuts for a season restored the soil's nitrates, but then farmers were left with an abundance of peanuts that no one really wanted. Rather than telling them to throw the peanuts away, Carver looked for new uses for the peanut. Years later, Carver described his scientific process in figuring out how to turn a throwaway plant into gold:

> Why, I just took a handful of peanuts and looked at them. "Great Creator," I said, "why did you make the peanut? Why?" With such knowledge as I had of chemistry and physics I

set to work to take the peanut apart. I separated the water, the fats, the oils, the gums, the resins, sugars, starches, pectoses, pentoses, pentosans, legumen, lysin, the amino, and amido acids. There! I had the parts of the peanut all spread out before me. Then I merely went on to try different combinations of those parts, under different conditions of temperature, pressure, and so forth.[4]

Through years of research, Carver came up with more than three hundred different uses for the peanut, turning what before had been rubbish into a bonanza of profitability for farmers. In fifty years of work at Tuskegee, George Washington Carver discovered more than five hundred different products that could be made from things commonly grown or found on Southern farms; many had previously been considered useless. In that time, he took out only three patents for these products, saying, "God gave them to me. How can I sell them to someone else?"

George Washington Carver literally spun peanuts into gold with nothing to invest but time and talent. He had a thirst for knowledge and was always willing to share it for "the price of a postage stamp." He was no ivory tower intellectual either. He spent much of his time spreading the gospel to any who would listen, speaking about the value of the love of science and the love of God. Carver advised:

> To those who have as yet not learned the secret of true happiness, which is the joy of coming into the closest relationship with the Maker and Preserver of all things: begin now to study the little things in your own door yard, going from the known to the nearest related unknown, for indeed each new truth brings one nearer to God.[5]

"Give Us This Day"

As you pray, "Give us this day our daily bread," let God infect your thoughts with His possibilities just as He did for men like George Washington Carver and R. G. LeTourneau, who through God's inspiration thought to put a blade on the front of a tractor to create the bulldozer. He was literally a "mover of mountains" as the primary designer of most of the earth-moving machinery we know of today. Such mountain movers take what is right in front of them—the arrows they had in their hands at the time—and strike repeatedly at their destinies until they've dug up the world-transforming ideas and inventions that God hid away "for such a time as theirs." They became tools of kingdom-building by being hungry enough to chase after knowledge and truth with all of their hearts.

It has often been said, "Today is the first day of the rest of your life," but it is also the first day of the rest of eternity—the rest of your existence with God. Are you waiting for your ship to come in? Well, guess what. It already has! All you will ever need for your prosperity—and pouring out a blessing on the earth—is already at your fingertips. Your "daily bread" is already in your hands. What are you going to do with it?

> Prayer and faith, the universal remedies against every want and every difficulty; and the nourishment of prayer and faith, God's Holy Word, helped me over all the difficulties.
>
> —George Müller[6]

6

FREEDOM FOR ALL

Disentangled, Unencumbered, Undaunted

And forgive us our debts, as we forgive our debtors.
—MATTHEW 6:12

*"Let each one of you speak truth with his neighbor," for
we are members of one another. "Be angry, and do not
sin": do not let the sun go down on your wrath, nor give
place to the devil....Let all bitterness, wrath, anger,
clamor, and evil speaking be put away from you, with
all malice. And be kind to one another, tenderhearted,
forgiving one another, even as God in Christ forgave you.*
—EPHESIANS 4:25–27, 31–32

YOU DON'T HAVE to dig too deeply into the Scriptures to discover that division hinders our prayers and unity amplifies them. Mark 11:24–25 advocates:

> Therefore I say to you, whatever things you ask when you pray, believe that you receive them, and you will have them. And whenever you stand praying, if you have anything against anyone, forgive him, that your Father in heaven may also forgive you your trespasses.

This seems to state that standing in forgiveness is a key essential for receiving "whatever things you ask." If this were not true, why would Jesus also advise:

> Therefore if you bring your gift [*in our case, praise and worship* (see Hebrews 13:15)] to the altar, and there remember that your brother has something against you, leave your gift there before the altar, and go your way. First be reconciled to your brother, and then come and offer your gift.
>
> —MATTHEW 5:23–24

And as Peter advised:

> Husbands, likewise, dwell with them [*your wives*] with understanding, giving honor to the wife, as to the weaker vessel, and as being heirs together of the grace of life, *that your prayers may not be hindered.*
> —1 Peter 3:7, emphasis added

Then on the other side, Jesus tells us:

> Again I say to you that if two of you agree on earth concerning anything that they ask, it will be done for them by My Father in heaven.
> —Matthew 18:19

And David tells us:

> Behold, how good and how pleasant it is for brethren to dwell together in unity.... For there the Lord commanded the blessing—life forevermore.
> —Psalm 133:1, 3

Note that God does not just bless this unity, but He *commands* a blessing upon it!

In other places, we see that the power of Pentecost came as believers were "with one accord in one place" (Acts 2:1). God showed up in Acts 4 only when "they raised their voice to God with one accord" (v. 24). Considering these things, is there anything more important on earth than nurturing our relationships and avoiding walls of division that could be erected between us?

TEARING DOWN BARRIERS

Of all the relationships in our lives, there is none more important than our relationship with God through Jesus Christ. From our youth, sin emerges in our lives through selfishness, pride, and stubbornness, no matter who we are. That has to be washed away for us to know God as we were created to know Him. We must come to Jesus, accept Him as Lord and Savior, and let Him be the Mediator between God and ourselves. (See 1 Timothy 2:5–6.)

This is why prayer is so important; it is the only way we as individuals can come into communication with Jesus in order to be reconnected with God. Religion would have us think we take certain steps to come to salvation: pray this prayer, join this church, memorize these scriptures, believe these things, don't believe those things, listen to certain preachers and teachers, etc., etc. But Jesus didn't come so that religion would be the buffer between God and man, but so that each of us as individuals could come to know God for ourselves.

Every great revival since the coming of Jesus Christ—the Reformation, the first and second Great Awakenings, the evangelical movement, the Pentecostal movement and charismatic renewal, etc.—started with that very premise. Someone realized from Scripture that there was a more genuine relationship to God available than was being taught in their society. Then they began praying to receive it.

We have seen this already in the story of Madame Jeanne Guyon, but she was far from alone in her experience. Another good example of this happened in the life of Charles Finney. As an apprentice lawyer in the office of Judge Benjamin Wright, Charles found that the Bible was quoted again and again as the justification for various laws. He had little interest in religion at the time, but was intrigued by the Bible as a foundational text for the US legal system and the laws of the state of New York, so he purchased a Bible and began to read it in his spare time.[1]

Finney became so engrossed in reading the Bible that he almost was ashamed. He would hide it under his law books in case anyone happened to come into his office. As a result, he began to wrestle with the question of salvation and approached it mentally as he would any other point he might argue in a court of law. The question of his own salvation consumed his thought life to the point that one day on the way to work, the following question popped into his mind: "What are you waiting for? Did you not promise to give your heart to God? And what are you trying to do? Are you endeavoring to work out a righteousness of your own?"[2]

In his *Memoirs*, Charles describes what followed that challenge from the Holy Spirit:

> Just at this point the whole question of Gospel salvation opened to my mind in a manner most marvellous to me at the time. I think I then saw, as clearly as I ever have in my life, the reality and

fullness of the atonement of Christ. I saw that his work was a finished work; and that instead of having, or needing, any righteousness of my own to recommend me to God, I had to submit myself to the righteousness of God through Christ....

Without being distinctly aware of it, I had stopped in the street right where the inward voice seemed to arrest me. How long I remained in that position, I cannot say. But after this distinct revelation had stood for some little time before my mind, the question seemed to be put, "Will you accept it now, to-day?" I replied, "Yes; I will accept it to-day, or I will die in the attempt."[3]

Turning on his heels at that point, Finney decided he would go into the woods north of the village of Adams and kneel there to pray until he knew he was saved, period. That was it. If God didn't save him, as far as he was concerned, he would never leave those woods again. Yet despite his resolve, prayer didn't come easily.

When I attempted to pray I found that my heart would not pray. I had supposed that if

I could only be where I could speak aloud, without being overheard, I could pray freely. But lo! When I came to try, I was dumb; that is, I had nothing to say to God; or at least I could say but a few words, and those without heart. In attempting to pray I would hear a rustling in the leaves, as I thought, and would stop and look up to see if somebody were not coming. This I did several times.

Finally I found myself verging fast to despair. I said to myself, "I cannot pray. My heart is dead to God, and will not pray." I then reproached myself for having promised to give my heart to God before I left the woods....My inward soul hung back, and there was no going out of my heart to God. I began to feel deeply that it was too late; that it must be that I was given up of God and was past hope....

Just at this moment I again thought I heard some one approach me, and I opened my eyes to see whether it were so. But right there the revelation of my pride of heart, as the great difficulty that stood in the way, was distinctly shown to me....It broke me down before the Lord.

Just at that point this passage of Scripture

seemed to drop into my mind with a flood of light: "Then shall ye go and pray unto me, and I will hearken unto you. Then shall ye seek me and find me, when ye shall search for me with all your heart." I instantly seized hold of this with my heart. I had intellectually believed the Bible before; but never had the truth been in my mind that faith was a voluntary trust instead of an intellectual state. I was as conscious as I was of my existence, of trusting at that moment in God's veracity. Somehow I knew that that was a passage of Scripture, though I do not think I had ever read it. I knew that it was God's word, and God's voice, as it were, that spoke to me. I cried to Him, "Lord, I take thee at thy word. Now thou knowest that I do search for thee with all my heart, and that I have come here to pray to thee; and thou hast promised to hear me."

That seemed to settle the question that I could then, that day, perform my vow. The Spirit seemed to lay stress upon that idea in the text, "When you search for me with all your heart." The question of when, that is of the present time, seemed to fall heavily into my heart. I told the Lord that I should take him at his word; that he could not lie; and that therefore I was sure that he heard my prayer, and that he would be found of me....

I continued thus to pray, and to receive and appropriate promises for a long time, I know not how long. I prayed till my mind became so full that, before I was aware of it, I was on my feet and tripping up the ascent toward the road. The question of my being converted, had not so much as arisen to my thought; but as I went up, brushing through the leaves and bushes, I recollect saying with great emphasis, "If I am ever converted, I will preach the Gospel."[4]

Charles was surprised to learn it was already lunchtime when he returned, but his life would never be the same again. As he searched his heart that day, he made a stunning realization: any sense of his unworthiness before God was gone. There was no more concern about whether he was saved or not, and in place of the anxiety that had previously kept him up nights was perfect peace.

We can never be real in any other relationship in our

lives if we are not real about our relationship with God. If we do not know God's forgiveness ourselves through faith and personal revelation, then how are we going to express true forgiveness to others? How are we truly going to resist judging others for their mistakes if we are still caught in the trap of wondering whether or not we are forgiven ourselves?

I cannot pray that prayer for you, but I can assure you that when Jesus instructed us to begin our prayers "our Father," it was because He wanted us to realize just how close God really is to us and how loving He is toward us. He wants us to know that when He has heard, the matter is settled. God's peace is not complacency. It is as possible for us to know our prayers are heard as it was for Charles Finney to know that he was saved. Yet do we persevere in prayer ourselves? Do we value our relationship with God more than life itself, as Finney did? Or are we sidetracked by doubts and distractions?

There is a certain degree of trial and error in coming to know God with this kind of surety. Too many give up on it or accept the teaching that knowing God in this way is only meant for a chosen few. Another problem is that in order to be close to God, we must walk a path that takes us out of ourselves and demands that we leave behind the baggage of hang-ups, doubt, self-centeredness, destructive habits, addictions, and hatred. Though the path is well marked, it is a journey we must master on our own. So many guides have pointed the way, but they cannot take our hand and lead us. Each step is up to us alone.

Not only that, but there is an agent working to see that we fail to reach the next level on the ascending path. He cannot take the path from us, but he can encourage us to lose our way. His greatest weapon is not so much deception as it is distraction. He always uses things—the cares of this world, the deceitfulness of riches, or our desire for the good things in life—to cause us to turn aside onto a winding rabbit trail that ultimately leads us nowhere. Most of these things are not evil in and of themselves, but God's kingdom must always be our first priority. Our other desires must come after that, otherwise they will become the very distractions that can get us lost. As Jesus said:

> Therefore do not worry, saying, "What shall we eat?" or "What shall we drink?" or "What shall we wear?" [*These are all concerns and desires of this world.*] For after all these things the Gentiles seek. For your heavenly Father knows that you need all these things. But seek first the kingdom of God and His righteousness, and all these things shall be added to you.
>
> —MATTHEW 6:31–33

We will not be able to forgive others until we truly know forgiveness for ourselves, and true forgiveness comes only at the feet of Jesus. This is why we should treasure this relationship above all others in our lives and even above life itself. This is the resolve that defines abiding in God, and that abiding is what brings the supernatural kingdom into the natural realm.

TRUE RICHES

The bigger the vision God gives you, the more likely it is that God has called others to work beside you in fulfilling it. It is likely, in fact, that you will not even be the leader in the endeavor. God commonly tests our dedication to His plan by seeing if we will be faithful in helping someone else accomplish the vision He has given him or her.

Too often we think of the tasks of establishing the kingdom and forget about the people along the way. We are all too willing to use and abuse people to get what we want or to accomplish what God is calling us to do. But it is important to remember that although achieving something great for the kingdom is extremely fulfilling, the riches are in the relationships we develop, not the institutions we build or the programs accredited to our names. To say it another way, the riches of the kingdom of God are its people, not its tabernacles. The only things from this earth that will last forever are the relationships we take with us into heaven.

Jesus even commends scoundrels who take care of their relationships first. Look at what He had to say about the man we have traditionally come to call the "unfaithful steward":

> There was a certain rich man who had a steward, and an accusation was brought to him that this man was wasting his goods. So he called him and said to him, "What is this I hear about you?

Give an account of your stewardship, for you can no longer be steward."

Then the steward said within himself, "What shall I do? For my master is taking the stewardship away from me. I cannot dig; I am ashamed to beg. I have resolved what to do, that when I am put out of the stewardship, they may receive me into their houses."

So he called every one of his master's debtors to him, and said to the first, "How much do you owe my master?" And he said, "A hundred measures of oil." So he said to him, "Take your bill, and sit down quickly and write fifty." Then he said to another, "And how much do you owe?" So he said, "A hundred measures of wheat." And he said to him, "Take your bill, and write eighty." So the master commended the unjust steward because he had dealt shrewdly. For the sons of this world are more shrewd in their generation than the sons of light.

And I say to you, *make friends for yourselves by unrighteous mammon*, that when you fail, they may receive you into an everlasting home.

—LUKE 16:1–9, EMPHASIS ADDED

Now this man was virtually stealing from his master. Is Jesus commending him for that? I don't think so! Look at what Jesus says about this man: *he used money to make friends*, to take burdens (of debt, in this case) off of others, and thus also increased the reputation of his master as a generous man.

Who are we but stewards of our Lord's provisions? We are His viceroys on the earth—appointed governors over the "realm" of our relationships, ambassadors of the kingdom of heaven who are equipped with time, talents, treasure, faith, and a growing knowledge of the God of the universe. We have access through prayer to the riches of heaven. So what do we do with that access? Do we build our own kingdoms or God's? Do we create our own places of luxury and comfort or ease the burdens of others? Do we cherish and appreciate (i.e., increase in value) our relationships, or do we sit back, look at all we have, and decide to "eat, drink, and be merry" (Luke 12:16–21)? These are tough questions, but the answers are all too telling.

Let me ask you another question while we are at this: Are you married? Outside of your relationship with God and your honesty with yourself, there is no more powerful relationship on the earth, yet many of us come to despise it. It isn't hard to look at statistics about the family and divorce and see that marriage is under attack. Why? It is very simple: "If two of you agree on earth concerning anything that they ask, it will be done for them by My Father in heaven" (Matt. 18:19). Imagine for a moment the unlimited power of a husband and wife who walk constantly in agreement! The power of a mother and father united in the raising of children who understand the power of relationships, are saturated in wisdom, and full of faith! How different would our world be today if there were more couples like this? How different would the church be? How different would our communities be? How different would our nations be?

Many speak out against gay marriage, homosexuality, and abortion as threats against our families, but these are truly just symptoms of diseased relationships, not causes. We have women trying to be men and men trying to be women, and we wonder why our churches are weak and our society corrupted. It is because we don't know how to find fulfillment in the sanctity of our marriages, let alone how to teach that to others. We cherish the physical benefits of marriage more than the spiritual ones and thus are willing to cheat to get the quick fix of sexual pleasure in ways God never intended us to need. We don't know how to meld our souls together in matrimony, so we argue over trivialities or, worse yet, lapse into our own private, selfish little worlds, living together physically like roommates but divided in heart, mind, and purpose.

It is not hard to realize, brothers and sisters, these things ought not to be.

Even more than charity, forgiveness must start at home. We can never afford to let the tiny bricks of resentment slowly mount up between us until we are living lives totally unto ourselves. We cannot afford to let issue after issue in our lives go neglected and unresolved until we are walking around on eggshells with our spouse, afraid to wake the five-hundred-pound gorilla of unresolved irritations sleeping in the corner of the room. We have to learn how to be angry and sin not—to fight fairly even concerning the issues we are most passionate about, dealing with our differences in ways that hold the relationship above our own needs for self-justification. This is how we break apart strongholds (2 Cor. 10:4–5), tear down walls of separation (Eph. 2:14), and truly become one in the unity of the Spirit and the bond of peace (Eph. 4:3). For if we can't do this in the relationships we have pledged our lives to, what hope is there for improving the other relationships in our families, in our workplaces or churches, across generations, or between ethnicities and cultures?

It has often been said that living with unforgiveness is like drinking poison and hoping the other person would die. Too many relationships in our midst have been poisoned in just such a way. I believe one of the reasons God created marriage is this: there is no better way to dig out these inner hurts and prejudices than by striving to be truly one spirit, soul, and body with someone who is likely your opposite in many ways. It just shows us all the more our need for a vital, thriving relationship with God. There are things that will only be exposed as we try to be one—things that are holding us back from all God wants for us, attitudes that are stumbling blocks, and prejudices that marriage so effortlessly exposes. This is why strong marriages are so important to the kingdom of

God and why it is so important for those of us who are not married to walk that much closer to Christ.

These principles apply to every relationship in our lives, though certainly to a lesser degree. If we have done the full internal work in our most intimate relationships, it is easier for us to be more transparent in our other relationships, which will make them more rewarding. It is much more effective to join in purpose with others for our work, social outreaches, or spreading of God's kingdom than to be constantly competing with one another. This is what the kingdom of God is all about. After all, proactive forgiveness in practice looks a lot like love.

THE REASON LOVE NEVER FAILS

Forgiving your debtors as God has forgiven you is 1 Corinthians 13 in action.

> Love suffers long and is kind; love does not envy; love does not parade itself, is not puffed up; does not behave rudely, does not seek its own, is not provoked, thinks no evil; does not rejoice in iniquity, but rejoices in the truth;

bears all things, believes all things, hopes all
things, endures all things. Love never fails.

—1 CORINTHIANS 13:4–8

Take a moment to look at that passage again, but
this time, in every place where it says "love," replace
that word with your name. That's you walking in
love. That's you walking in proactive forgiveness.
That's you cherishing your relationships over your
things; over your accomplishments, goals, and tasks;
and over yourself. That's you living the richest life
possible. It is also a foundational component of living
the impossible life Jesus has called us to live in His
image. It is faith at work and the key to doing the
"greater works" (John 14:12) our world needs to
manifest God's kingdom.

> Spirituality without a prayer life is no
> spirituality at all, and it will not last beyond
> the first defeats. Prayer is an opening of the
> self so that the Word of God can break in and
> make us new. Prayer unmasks. Prayer converts.
> Prayer impels. Prayer sustains us on the way.

Pray for the grace it will take to continue what
you would like to quit.

—Joan D. Chittister[5]

7

THIS DAY I WILL
Two Steps Forward, No Steps Back

And do not lead us into temptation, but deliver us from the evil one.
—Matthew 6:13

Do not be overcome by evil, but overcome evil with good.
—Romans 12:21

TODAY HAS A place in eternity that no other day can take. There are things God has established for you to accomplish this day, and there are things the devil has set up to distract you. Certainly there is some leeway in this, and God gives an incredible amount of grace, but what we do with today matters, not only for ourselves but also for those God has appointed for us to touch. Satan, on the other hand, would like to sideline us permanently, derail the will of God, and interfere with the formation of His kingdom.

Temptation comes to do just these things. The Greek term for *sin* literally means, "to miss the mark…[to] wander from the path of uprightness and honor, to do or go wrong."[1] The term has often been used in reference to archery as a means of measuring by how much the shooter missed the bull's-eye or how short of the target the arrow fell.

We often associate sin only with great moral transgression, which in many ways is a method of self-justification: "Well, I've never committed adultery, robbed a bank, or killed someone, so I can't be that bad of a person." But sin is not just about great moral failure; it is more about the general failure of fulfilling our mission and assignment from God. Look at what the writer of Hebrews says about temptation and the race God has called us to run:

> Let us lay aside every weight, and the sin which so easily ensnares us, and let us run with endurance the race that is set before us, looking unto Jesus, the author and finisher of our faith, who for the joy that was set before Him endured the cross, despising the shame, and has sat down at the right hand of the throne of God.
> —Hebrews 12:1–2

He sets Jesus as our example. Jesus was without sin because He knew that even one small sin would have defeated Him in the race His Father set before Him. And because Jesus lived without sin, we have access to the forgiveness of our sins and therefore have the ability to run the race God has set before us unencumbered by their entanglements. As we ask for that fresh forgiveness every day and determine to live in proactive forgiveness, we must also determine that we will not let distractions, selfishness, poor self-control, foolish decisions, or other "sins" keep us from the mark God has set for each of us.

Satan would inch us off the track of our destiny so minutely and, perhaps, unnoticeably that over time getting back to fulfilling our God-given purpose will seem monumental because of the mistakes we have made. However, if we correct course each day and keep our hearts open to God's correction in each moment, we can stay on track. Resisting temptation is not to deny living or the joys of life, as the devil would have us believe. It is disciplining ourselves to win the race God has called us to win. And sometimes it is not so much about the things we don't do, but more about keeping busy doing the things we should do.

No runner getting ready for a marathon would fasten heavy diver's weights around her ankles as she prepares to start her race. Nor does she put on heavy blue jeans and a thick, winter jacket. Instead she dresses as lightly and sleekly as she can, ready to run for hours without stopping. In our lives as Christians called to dismantle the kingdom of darkness and establish the kingdom of light, we need to prepare ourselves and train for the marathons God has set before us—and not just for the short sprints we would prefer to run and be done with.

Thousands may gather in the arena to watch the end of a marathon and cheer on the participants, but training begins in obscurity. No one is around when the runners rise at 5:00 a.m. to get in a five-mile run before breakfast. In the same way, the crowds don't gather as we get up earlier than normal to have more time for prayer, Bible reading, and listening in on the big conversation of God's plans and directives for the day. This is the place we prepare for the race God has called us to, lightening the load by stripping away the bad habits and weaknesses that would trip us up, and putting on the love and grace that will strengthen us throughout the day.

It is where we grow in maturity, wisdom, and endurance to be able to handle whatever the race might throw at us, and to recommit ourselves to the author and finisher of our faith, the Alpha and Omega of our race. We must prepare today when the pressures on us are light so we will be able to face the tougher legs of the race with grace and courage. Overcomers are not born; they are developed over time, and prayer is the place that development takes place.

PUTTING OFF ENCUMBRANCES

I believe this is why Jesus told His disciples that some challenges would be too great for them unless they first had spent a good deal of time in "prayer and fasting" (Matt. 17:21). However, very few today understand the true power and function of fasting. They think of it merely as going hungry for a time as an act of devotion to God or a way of "cleansing their temple" of unwanted weight or impurities. The devil would make it just one more meaningless practice of a confusing faith. But that was not God's purpose for fasting, nor was it why everyone from Moses to Jesus to Paul fasted. To benefit from fasting, we must understand its true purpose and role in living life by the Spirit and not the flesh.

At its heart, fasting is faith in action—faith that says, "Spiritual things are more substantial than physical things, even down to the most basic of human appetites and hungers." We are not spiritual beings by default; we must choose to live by the Spirit rather than be ruled by the things our physical senses and desires tell us we need. It is fasting that says, "Man shall not live by bread alone, but by every word that proceeds from the mouth of God" (Matt. 4:4)—just as Jesus did when He went into the wilderness before He began His ministry. It is disciplining the body to be in obedience to the Spirit in all things.

You have to understand that fasting is not just about food, though food is perhaps the most primal and demanding of our physical needs. Try to go without food for twenty-four, thirty-six, or seventy-two hours— or just skip a meal—and see if your body doesn't say something about it. I guarantee that the minute you make the decision to fast, your stomach will have something to say about it. Your stomach will likely start complaining just minutes after you enter your closet to pray.

If you can discipline your willpower by going without food for a time in order to receive the "bread" of God's Word, what "appetite" couldn't you overcome? If you can go without eating to chase after God, then can't you also go without television, texting, talking too long on the phone, surfing the Internet, picking at meaningless tasks, playing video games without end, criticizing others, letting defeating thoughts have the final say, or any of the myriad of other things that are holding you back from God's will and purpose for your life?

You see, fasting is not primarily about denying yourself food; anyone can do that for any of a hundred different reasons. It is about disciplining yourself to overcome cravings and demands so that when you meet a hardship in your God-given mission, you will prevail over it. It is about resisting distraction. It is about overcoming the power of addiction—and I am not just talking about drugs and alcohol here. I am talking about the little foxes that aren't really "wrong" per se—things we wouldn't normally classify as "sin" but that will hold you back from being all you should be in Christ. It is about overcoming and denying those things that come between you and your time with God in prayer and Scripture reading. It is about choosing God's power and ways over the concerns of the world; about living a life that is uncompromising yet loving and forgiving. It is about pruning from your life the habits that will keep you from being who God has called you to be. As Andrew Murray put it:

> We are creatures of the senses: our mind is helped by what comes to us embodied in concrete form; fasting helps to express, to deepen, and to confirm the resolution that we are ready to sacrifice anything, to sacrifice ourselves, to attain what we seek for the kingdom of God.[2]

How do you know what those things are—what things you should be fasting from? Easy. When you think about going off by yourself to read your Bible and pray, what are the things that come to mind and get in the way? Which things consume large chunks of time that would be better investing elsewhere? Is it, "Oh, let me just check my e-mail first," or, "You know what, my favorite show is on. I'll watch that first, then I will go and pray." Or is it, "OK, let me just go get a snack and then I will open my Bible," or, "Oh, Lord, not before I get my coffee!"

What is it that possesses your thoughts as you go through the day? What is it that takes you out of prayerfulness? Whatever it is, perhaps that is the thing you should be "fasting" from even more than food!

Prayer is not just a place of laying our petitions before heaven and lifting up God's holy name in praise and worship. It is also a place of being refined and broken and remolded. It is where we come before the Lord to be pruned of the habits, desires, and ambitions that would hinder all God has for us. It is the furnace where the impurities are refined out of the gold of our lives.

Through fasting we deny the natural world's domination over us and amplify our allegiance to God, who must be worshiped in *spirit* and in truth. After all, humanity first fell because we gave into a physical hunger—because Adam and Eve couldn't resist eating a natural food that appealed to their physical eyes even if it meant breaking a supernatural commandment. The first temptation of Jesus was that He should break His fast and turn stones into bread. Like Him, we are to deny the power of physical food to distract us from banqueting on God's Word. This is the starting place to resisting the other temptation Jesus would face—twisting the Word of God for His own glory or building His own kingdom rather than His Father's. (See Matthew 4:1–11.)

Fasting was also meant to lead to loving action. Jesus fasted to gain the strength to begin His ministry upon the earth. Paul fasted for the supernatural revelation that would deliver the Gentiles. It is a disciplining of self in preparation of doing the work and will of God. As Paul described the process:

> Do you not know that those who run in a race all run, but one receives the prize? Run in such a way that you may obtain it. And everyone who competes for the prize is temperate in all things. Now they do it to obtain a perishable crown, but we for an imperishable crown. Therefore I run thus: not with uncertainty. Thus I fight: not as one who beats the air. But I discipline my body and bring it into subjection, lest, when I have preached to others, I myself should become disqualified.
>
> —1 CORINTHIANS 9:24–27

Fasting is thus a part of every life hungry for more of God. It is not to be an empty practice aimed only at increasing our own willpower, for what is willpower if it is not set to work establishing God's kingdom? What is faith if it is not expressed in love? Great faith is only expressed in great works—and great works are defined only by the love they express. So, just as with our prayers, there is to be an aim and a purpose to our fasting—namely love. As God expressed it through the prophet Isaiah:

> This is the kind of fast day I'm after: to break the chains of injustice, get rid of exploitation in the workplace, free the oppressed, cancel debts. What I'm interested in seeing you do is: sharing your food with the hungry, inviting the homeless poor into your homes, putting clothes on the shivering ill-clad, being available to your own families. Do this and the lights will turn on, and your lives will turn around at once.
> —ISAIAH 58:6–8, THE MESSAGE

Fasting is the putting away of distractions and entangling habits so that we can be freer to work in love. Look at the example left to us by Daniel, Hananiah, Mishael, and Azariah. (See Daniel 1–2.) Captured as children and taken to Babylon, they were selected for a special program by King Nebuchadnezzar. They were to be educated in the culture and religion of the Babylonians and become servants in the king's house. As part of their daily provision, they would be given the same delicacies as the king received at his table, many of which violated Hebrew dietary laws. To keep themselves pure, these four Hebrew youths fasted, eating only vegetables and water. Upon a challenge that they would not be as healthy as the other servants because of their restricted diets, after a ten-day test period "their features appeared better and fatter in flesh than all the young men who ate the portion of the king's delicacies" (Dan. 1:15).

Yet not only were they healthier, but as they grew up living this "fasted" lifestyle, their spiritual power to interpret dreams and visions and withstand persecution was like that of no other person in the Old Testament. When Nebuchadnezzar had a prophetic dream, not only could they tell him the meaning of the dream, but they also knew what the dream was without being told. Some of the most profound prophecies of the Second

Coming of Jesus Christ were given to Daniel for him to record.

Of all the stories of the Bible, Daniel and his friends were among those who showed the purest character and integrity. Nothing negative is recorded of Daniel, which is something that cannot be said for anyone else in the Bible except Jesus and John the Baptist. In Ezekiel 14, when the greatest intercessors of all time are mentioned, Daniel is prominent on the list alongside Noah and Job (vv. 14, 20). It is quite possible the three Hebrew children might have died in the fiery furnace of Nebuchadnezzar had they not had the spiritual power obtained through a lifetime of devotion marked by regular fasting.

If your first thought in kneeling down to pray is that you need to go get something to eat before you start, check your e-mails or text messages, or look up something on the Internet, then you may have struck upon the very thing you should fast for a few days or a few weeks. Replace the time you would have spent on that activity with prayer. Then see what happens. I believe that as you do this, your faith will be renewed. You will find your "first love" for God being rejuvenated, and you will step further into the life God has been trying to give you since you first gave Him your heart. It will begin stretching what you can trust God for and what you can accomplish in Him.

The Faith That Grows

The "stretch" of faith in our lives should never really change. As we grow in God so should the capacity of what we can accomplish in Christ. As our faith grows, so should the magnitude of our dreams and what we are asking God to do. In this way, our faith is constantly reaching out for things that are just beyond our natural ability to gasp them. For George Müller, it was just as difficult to believe for a five-pound note as it was years later for him to believe God would provide for the care and feeding of two thousand orphans. His faith had grown along with the level of his need.

There is a problem when we settle into the comfort zone of our gifts and purpose. When God calls us, He also supernaturally equips us with spiritual abilities in line with that divine mission and assignment. Regardless of whether we pursue God's glory in that purpose or our own, those divine gifts and abilities will still function in our lives, "for the gifts and the calling of God are irrevocable" (Rom. 11:29). Thus it is possible to do great things and even see miracles happen in *our* ministries, yet miss God by never continuing to *stretch* after Him. If this were not true, how would it be possible for Jesus to say:

> Not everyone who says to Me, "'Lord, Lord,'" shall enter the kingdom of heaven, but he who does the will of My Father in heaven. Many will say to Me in that day, "Lord, Lord, have we not prophesied in Your name, cast out demons in Your name, and done many wonders in Your name?" And then I will declare to them, "*I never knew you*; depart from Me, you who practice lawlessness!"
>
> —MATTHEW 7:21–23, EMPHASIS ADDED

"I called you, I anointed you, I equipped you, but I never *knew* you." Can you imagine what it would be like to hear those words when you finally get to meet Jesus face-to-face? But this is the outcome we risk if we try to do the will of God without seeking the face of God—if we settle into the comfortable pattern of doing the work of the Lord without getting our daily instructions from the Lord of the work. This is to inch our way off the path God has set before us without anyone ever realizing it. It is to despise the greatness of what God wants to do through us for the compromise of living well enough as we are, for settling into a life without growth.

Praying daily not to be led into temptation and to be delivered from evil is to center each day in the will of God and focus on the good you will do—the step-by-step righting of evil in our world without slipping back into old habits or complacent attitudes. Circumstances can bring setbacks, but with God, what the devil meant for evil will be turned on its head into good. We must open our ears to hear what needs to be covered in prayer for the protection of ourselves, our families, those within our realm of influence, and the missions to which God has assigned us and our churches.

If every day we are following God closely in the tenets of the disciple's prayer, then we are becoming dangerous to evil, and evil will want to become dangerous to us. However, if we stay clothed in the armor of Christ, we are protected. We man our posts, follow our orders, and thus keep temptations from tripping us up or selfishness from entering our hearts and sending us off course. It is the only way to triumph in the mission and purpose God has called us to—and to one day hear, "Well done, My good and faithful steward."

> Pray as if everything depended on God and work as if everything depended on you.
> —St. Ignatius of Loyola[3]

8

VICTORY!

Fear in the Enemies' Eyes

For Yours is the kingdom and the power
and the glory forever. Amen.
—MATTHEW 6:13

He who overcomes, and keeps My works until the
end, to him I will give power over the nations.
—REVELATION 2:26

As the bus boycott in Montgomery, Alabama, was beginning to garner national attention in 1956, Martin Luther King Jr. was just settling into bed after a long, hard day. His wife, Coretta, was already asleep. Just then the phone rang. He picked it up without thinking of the hour to hear, "Listen, [expletive], we've taken all we want from you; before next week you'll be sorry you ever came to Montgomery."[1]

Dr. King was speechless, but it didn't matter. The line had already gone dead. Settling the receiver back into its cradle, he felt the fear and tension of all of the previous months of battle for respect and civil rights well up in his throat. He'd heard such threats before, but now it was as if the weight of all of them came crashing down on him at once. There was no going back to sleep. His heart was in turmoil.

Eventually he found himself in the kitchen where he heated up a pot of coffee, but after pouring a cup it just sat there untouched before him on the table. His thoughts wandered to his infant daughter sleeping in the next room. For the sake of her gentle little smile and the safety of his family, was there a way to get out of this movement before things got ugly? Could he really ask his family to go through this kind of madness day in and day out for who knew how long? Could he risk losing them? Or them losing him?

Something inside of him said, "You can't call on Daddy now, you can't even call on Mama. You've got to call on that something in that person that your Daddy used to tell you about, that power that can make a way out of no way."[2]

He bowed his head into his hands at the kitchen table and prayed, "Lord, I'm down here trying to do what's right. I think I'm right. I am here taking a stand for what I believe is right. But, Lord, I must confess that I'm weak now. I'm faltering. I'm losing my courage. Now, I am afraid. And I can't let the people see me like this because if they see me weak and losing my courage, they will begin to get weak. The people are looking to me for leadership, and if I stand before them without strength and courage, they too will falter. I am at the end of my powers. I have nothing left. I've come to the point where I can't face it alone."[3]

And then almost immediately from within himself, he heard, "Martin Luther, stand up for righteousness. Stand up for justice. Stand up for truth. And lo, I will be with you. Even until the end of the world." The presence of God filled that quaint little kitchen and with it came the strength to push on. Fear disappeared in the presence of God's perfect love.[4]

Three nights later, as Dr. King was at a Monday evening prayer meeting, his wife and a friend from the church who was sitting with her heard a thump on the porch of the King home. It sounded like someone had thrown a brick at the front door, and then an explosion boomed as the bomb ignited on the porch. When Dr. King heard of the incident, he rushed home to find an angry crowd forming in his front yard as African Americans and police seemed at the point of forming battle lines and opening fire upon one another. The air was thick with the tension of distrust and the desire for blood to avenge this attack on Dr. King and his family, even if those they attacked had little to do with what happened. Racial differences were justification enough for many in the crowd.

After Dr. King was able to verify no one in his home had been hurt, he emerged onto the blackened porch to address the crowd:

We believe in law and order. Don't get panicky. Don't do anything panicky at all. Don't get your weapons. He who lives by the sword will perish by the sword. Remember that is what God said. We are not advocating violence. We want to love our enemies. I want you to love our enemies. Be good to them. Love them and let them know you love them.

I did not start this boycott. I was asked by you to serve as your spokesman. I want it known the length and breadth of this land that if I am stopped this movement will not stop. If I am stopped our work will not stop. For what we are doing is right. What we are doing is just. And God is with us.[5]

Just as in a Sunday morning address, he heard voices here and there in the crowd assuring him that they were with him and there would be no violence. Tensions dissipated almost instantly, and the crowd began to disperse.

Had Dr. King not heard those words in his kitchen a few nights earlier, would things have gone differently when his home was attacked? The fight of that civil rights leader might have ended that night instead of years later as the battle was nearly won. Had he not heard those words in prayer that night, who knows how different our world might be today.

What words should you be hearing from God to change your world, your nation, your city? How much are you willing to lay on the line that God's kingdom might be manifest in your midst?

It is one thing to preach the gospel in our congregations and see people come to know Jesus, and it is quite another to bring salvation in its every aspect to our neighborhoods and communities. To truly establish the kingdom of God on the earth is likely to take concentrated lifetimes; however, if we will apply the diligence of a William Wilberforce or a Dr. King, God will let us see victories—major victories—in our lifetimes. Are we willing to pay the price in time spent in prayer to see these things happen? Will we do today what is necessary for our children to live in a better tomorrow?

In a world often filled with corruption and hatred, we have a great deal of work to do for God's will to be available to all. The call for social justice as well as a renewed transformational empowerment of the gospel message is crucial for the course correction needed. Certainly we must hold forth the full gospel of Jesus Christ and the power of what He did on the cross as the doorway to the kingdom of God. But is it enough for people to just stumble across the portal and *see* the kingdom of heaven? Should we not also take hold of all that salvation means and *enter* into it as well? (See John 3:3, 5.)

It will take the daily prayers of dedicated Christians everywhere for the body of Christ to become the catalyst for positive change Jesus has called it to be. It is from the manifested "bubbles" of God's presence, which are invited to the earth through prayer, that the kingdom of God becomes evident within our lives to touch the lives of others. Those manifestations of His presence are where we receive vision from heaven of how things should be. And as we meditate on the things God downloads into our spirits, His divine strategies, wisdom, and inner resolve grow in our lives. These enable us to walk out His plans on the earth for accomplishing His purpose and calling for our lives.

It is one thing to hear from heaven, but will we *do*

what it takes to walk out our mission and assignments each and every day? Jesus never said that we would be judged by what we say we believe, but by the fruits of the actions dictated by what we truly do believe. (See Matthew 7:15–21.) As Andrew Murray taught, there can be no idle, unpraying hands if the harvest is to be gathered:

> Every believer is a laborer. As God's children, we have been redeemed for service and have our work waiting. It must be our prayer that the Lord would fill all His people with the spirit of devotion, so that no one may be found standing idle in the vineyard. Wherever there is a complaint about the lack of fit helpers for God's work, prayer has the promise of a supply.[6]

From discipline and wise strategy come victory, both on the battlefield and in the overall war. If we are properly plugging into prayer and hearing God's voice in relation to each day, we are plugging into the kingdom, power, and glory that are forever God's alone. Making faithful self-sacrifice by laying aside ourselves and praying for others leads to promotion, greater mission, and more profound influence. This is our victory in Him. How we walk in that victory determines the legacy we leave for the next generation.

Being all God has called you to be begins and ends in prayer. It is in hearing from heaven—plugging into the big conversation—that God's will for the earth today will be communicated to His people and put into action. Are you part of the fight to manifest God's kingdom of wholeness, freedom, and sufficiency? Are you a spreader of "righteousness and peace and joy in the Holy Spirit" (Rom. 14:17) for every race, creed, culture, and community?

It is my firm conviction that God has big plans for you and is waiting—literally knocking at the door (Rev. 3:20)—in order to meet with you and talk about your future and what you need to do today to prepare for it. Spend time in prayer today exercising your spiritual senses and learning to discern God's voice. The world is waiting for the manifestation of the sons and daughters of God. (See Romans 8:19–22.) It is time for us to step up and be the emissaries of God's goodness. It won't be easy, but it will be worth it. We have God's Word on it. It's time to unleash His kingdom so all of humanity will know the power of love and wisdom as it is manifested in the lives of those who belong to Him.

> The renewal of the Church will depend on the renewal of our prayer life. The powers of the world to come are at our disposal if we will make time for quiet hours for fellowship and communion [with Jesus in prayer], which is our Lord's supreme yearning desire.
>
> —FRANCIS A. McGAW[7]

NOTES

PREFACE

1. Mother Teresa, *Everything Starts From Prayer* (Ashland, OR: White Cloud Press, Second Edition, 2010), 1.
2. Edward McKendree Bounds, *Purpose in Prayer* (New York: Fleming H. Revell Company, 1920), 2.
3. Andrew Murray, *With Christ in the School of Prayer* (Radford, VA: Wilder Publications, 2008), 8–9.

INTRODUCTION

1. Murray, *With Christ in the School of Prayer*, 10.

CHAPTER 1
THE GREAT PARADIGM SHIFT

1. Pete Greig, "John—We Are a People of Destiny," sermon presented at 24-7 Prayer International's Feast 2007 in Seville, Spain, October 2007, 30:46.
2. As quoted by Rustin Carlson, "The Malachi Mandate," *Orphanology*, http://rustincarlson.blogspot.com/2010/10/campus-america-is-on-its-final-leg-of.html (accessed May 31, 2011).
3. Murray, *With Christ in the School of Prayer*, 196–197.
4. Gary Haugen, *Just Courage* (Downers Grove, IL: InterVarsity Press, 2008), 23.
5. Charles H. Spurgeon, "Effective Prayer," PreachtheWord.com, http://www.preachtheword.com/sermon/effectiveprayer.shtml (accessed April 18, 2011).

Chapter 2
First Things First

1. George Müller, *The Life of Trust: Being a Narrative of the Lord's Dealings with George Müller, Written by Himself* (Boston: Gould and Lincoln, 1867).

2. Ibid, 39.

3. Ibid, 39.

4. George Müller, A *Narrative of Some of the Lord's Dealings with George Müller. Written by Himself. First Part* (London: J. Nisbit & Company, 1860), 18.

5. Ibid, 37.

6. Ed Reese, *The Life and Ministry of George Mueller*, Christian Hall of Fame Series no. 23 (Lansing, IL: Reese Publications, n.d.), http://www.believersweb.org/view.cfm?ID=177 (accessed September 14, 2010).

7. Müller, *The Life of Trust: Being a Narrative of the Lord's Dealings with George Müller, Written by Himself*, 357.

8. Müller, *A Narrative of Some of the Lord's Dealings with George Müller. Written by Himself. First Part*, 144–146.

9. Müller, *The Life of Trust: Being a Narrative of the Lord's Dealings with George Müller, Written by Himself*, 113.

10. Brother Lawrence, *The Practice of the Presence of God: The Best Rule of Holy Life* (Peabody, MA: Hendrickson Publishers, 2004), ix.

11. Ibid., 20.

Chapter 3
What Should Be

1. Warren Buffett quote, *New York Magazine*, http://nymag.com/daily/intel/2009/06/you_cant_make_a_baby_in_a_mont.html, or Hark.com, http://www.hark.com/clips/wwtcbxqhzy-getting-9-women-pregnant (accessed April 19, 2011).

2. Greig, "John—We Are a People of Destiny."

3. Jeanne Guyon, *The Unabridged Collected Works of Jeanne Guyon* (n.p.: Kahley House Publishing, 2006).

4. Ibid.

5. Ibid. 299.

6. James Melvin Washington, *Conversations With God: Two Centuries of Prayers by African Americans* (New York: HarperCollins Publishers, Inc., 1994), 39.

Chapter 4
Mission: Impossible

1. Stephen Tomkins, *William Wilberforce: A Biography* (Oxford: Lion, 2007).

2. Robert Isaac and Samuel Wilberforce (eds.), *The Correspondence of William Wilberforce*, Volume 1 (London: John Murray, 1838), 149, in Clifford Hill, *The Wilberforce Connection* (London, England and Grand Rapids, MI: Monarch Books, 2004), 49.

3. Jonathan Aitken, "Foreword," in John Piper, *Amazing Grace in the Life of William Wilberforce* (Wheaton, IL: Crossway Books, 2006), 13–14.

4. Hill, *The Wilberforce Connection*, 64.

5. Michael Hennell, "William Wilberforce: The Clapham Sect," Church Society website, (2003), http://www.churchsociety .org/issues_new/history/wilberforce/iss_history_wilberforce_ hennell-claphamsect.asp (accessed October 25, 2010).

6. Norman Grubb, *Rees Howells: Intercessor* (Fort Washington, PA: CLC Publications, 1997).

7. Adapted from W. E. Vine, Merrill F. Unger, and William White, *Vine's Complete Expository Dictionary of Old and New Testament Words*, 2:369 (Nashville: T. Nelson, 1996).

8. *The Book of Eli*, directed by Albert Hughes and Allen Hughes (2010; Burbank, CA: Warner Home Video, 2010), DVD.

9. James Strong, *Enhanced Strong's Lexicon* (Ontario: Woodside Bible Fellowship, 1996), G1018.

10. John Wesley, "Plain Account of Christian Perfection," *The Works of the Reverend John Wesley, AM*, John Emory (ed.), (New York: T. Mason and G. Lane, 1839), 526.

CHAPTER 5
ENOUGH

1. Strong, *Enhanced Strong's Lexicon*, G841.

2. Edwin Louis Cole, as quoted in *Life's Ultimate To ~~Do~~ Be List* (Colorado Springs, CO: Honor Books, 2004), 87.

3. John S. Ferrell, *Fruits of Creation: A Look at Global Sustainability as Seen Through the Eyes of George Washington Carver* (Shakopee, MN: Macalester Park Publishing Company, 1995).

4. Ibid, 50.

5. Gary R. Kremer, ed., *George Washington Carver: In His Own Words* (Columbia, MO: The University of Missouri Press, 1987), 143.

6. Müller, *The Life of Trust: Being a Narrative of the Lord's Dealings with George Müller, Written by Himself.*

CHAPTER 6
FREEDOM FOR ALL

1. Charles G. Finney, *Memoirs of Reverend Charles G. Finney: Written by Himself* (New York: A. S. Barnes and Company, 1876).

2. Ibid, 14.

3. Ibid, 14.

4. Ibid, 15–17.

5. From *In a High Spiritual Season*, as quoted by Richard A. Kauffman in "Benedictine Wisdom," *Christianity Today*, December 29, 2008, http://www.christianitytoday.com/ct/2008/december/22.55.html (accessed April 20, 2011).

Chapter 7
This Day I Will

1. Strong, *Enhanced Strong's Lexicon*, G266.
2. Murray, *With Christ in the School of Prayer*, 99.
3. Catechism of the Catholic Church, Second Edition, No. 2834, http://www.scborromeo.org/ccc/p4s2a3.htm#2834 (accessed May 18, 2011).

Chapter 8
Victory!

1. Adapted from Clayborne Carson, ed., *The Autobiography of Martin Luther King, Jr.* (New York: Warner Books, 1998), chapter 8, http://mlk-kpp01.stanford.edu/index.php/kingpapers/article/chapter_8_the_violence_of_desperate_men/ (accessed July 28, 2011).
2. Ibid.
3. Ibid.
4. Ibid.
5. Ibid.
6. Murray, *With Christ in the School of Prayer*, 42.
7. E. G. Carre, ed., *Praying Hyde: The Life Story of John Hyde* (Orlando: Bridge Logos, 1982), 38.

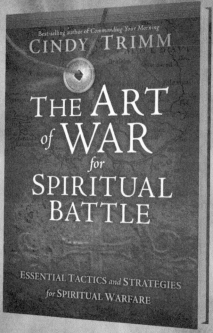